To John a

Love

Derek

Derek was born in 1951 in Aberdeen, Scotland. In 1955, he got his first tricycle. In 1956, he went to his first football match on his own using his tricycle. In 1969, he had progressed to another form of transport and became a bus conductor.

By 1975, he still had the travelling bug and moved to South Africa! In 1978 he returned to Britain to settle in the Lake District to bring up the family. In 2006, newly retired and having finally got rid of the kids, he at last had some free time to mess around in boats.

FREE TIME JOURNAL

Derek L Porteous

FREE TIME JOURNAL

Vanguard Press

VANGUARD PAPERBACK

© Copyright 2009
Derek L Porteous

The right of Derek L Porteous to be identified as author of this work has been asserted by him in accordance with the Copyright, Designs and Patents Act 1988.

All Rights Reserved

No reproduction, copy or transmission of this publication may be made without written permission.
No paragraph of this publication may be reproduced, copied or transmitted save with the written permission of the publisher, or in accordance with the provisions of the Copyright Act 1956 (as amended).

Any person who commits any unauthorised act in relation to this publication may be liable to criminal prosecution and civil claims for damages.

A CIP catalogue record for this title is available from the British Library.

ISBN 978 184386 498 1

Vanguard Press is an imprint of
Pegasus Elliot MacKenzie Publishers Ltd.
www.pegasuspublishers.com

First Published in 2009

Vanguard Press
Sheraton House Castle Park
Cambridge England

Printed & Bound in Great Britain

Dedication

To: Pam, Brian, Sandra and Garry

Introduction

There is nothing quite like messing around in boats. Ever since *Howard's Way* on television, I always quite liked the idea of sailing the seven seas in a nice shiny plastic sailing boat. So, at the ripe old age of 40 years old, I bought a 30ft sailing yacht and had it delivered to the west coast of Cumbria. My priorities were to decide on a name and, oh, learn how to sail. My wife, Pam, suggested *Free Time*. So, having christened our new pride and joy with a little champagne over her bow, and having quaffed the rest of the bottle, it was almost "job done". Then came the learning to sail bit...

After a few years on the rough and ready (big tides, long distances, rough seas) Irish Sea, we retreated to the relatively tranquil west coast of Scotland. Lurking around the back of my mind was an unformulated, and certainly unmentioned, plan to circumnavigate the Mediterranean. After a few years, this plan was downgraded to a quick whiz around the British Isles, and perhaps Ireland. Now like most unformulated, and unmentioned, plans, there were a number of flaws. These flaws are in no particular order, but each one was a show-stopper. Although I was very proud of *Free Time*, a 30ft yacht is exceedingly uncomfortable. It had no AC electricity, no hot water, no heating and, let's face it, is very primitive. Pam got violently seasick in anything above a gentle breeze and then refused to allow *Free Time* to hoist her white flappy things. *Free Time* the sailing yacht was effectively emasculated, despite being a "she". Finally, we were both working, and our respective employers did want to see us at regular intervals, hopefully at nine o'clock each morning.

Having failed miserably on sailing Plan A, I then began to think about sailing Plan B. Obviously we had to keep messing about on boats, but perhaps the other slight issues could be resolved.

Since early childhood, I was always fascinated with what was around the corner. Nothing as grandiose as "what is the next stage of my life?" What twists and turns in fate would see me on the road to fame and fortune? "No, it was literally what was around the corner? Where did the road in front of our house go to? Did it lead to the football pitch or, perhaps, a corner shop with sweets in the window?" This inane sense of curiosity heightened when I substituted the railway for the road. There was something comforting about the narrow restriction of the rail track and, perversely, the lack of numerous options in terms of decisions of which way to go. You either went up track, or down track. Occasionally the choice of a branch line would present itself, but those were few and far between, unlike the road system which threw up choices at every road intersection. Erich Fromm was right with his "Fear of Freedom" theory. It certainly scared me. I did not want the freedom to turn left or right every ten minutes or so; I wanted a restricted, predetermined narrow path.

Now I could not afford a hulking great locomotive with associated carriages, and I guess Richard Branson might object if I stopped on the Glasgow to London track somewhere quiet for a cup of tea. But hold on, translate this childish objective, add a little messing about in boats, and what do you get? A narrowboat and the inland waterway system, that's what you get.

Plan B was becoming clearer. This time I thought it wise to vocalise the plan. After all, I was expecting Pam to join me, so I guess she needed to know, and approve, at some stage, otherwise who would cook breakfast? Surprisingly Pam readily agreed. She even went as far as to say, "That is a good idea."

So *Free Time* the plastic yacht was sold, and *Free Time*, the steel narrowboat was ordered. At the time, there was a year's waiting list from all the major builders. This suited my timetable, so a deposit winged its way to our builder, Liverpool Boats, and we joined the queue. Two years later (narrowboat builders are never on time) a second bottle of champagne was duly dribbled over the bow. We took delivery of our second *Free Time*. She was a beautiful 55ft steel narrowboat. She had an all-wood interior, a fixed double bed, hot water, TV, washing machine, central heating, and, joy of joys, a proper flushing toilet.

So Plan B was overcoming the fatal flaws in Plan A. We had a comfortable boat, on which we could happily live for months at a time. Even Pam could not claim to get seasick on the mirror-still canal waters. All we needed now was time to live the dream.

Our two sons, Brian and Garry, had completed their university education and had long flown the nest. In fact Brian had carried on flying for longer than expected to eventually land in Sydney, Australia. We did visit each year, but Pam and my respective holiday allowances from our employers permitted only a couple of weeks. It didn't take long to realise that we needed to take early retirement. This freed up the summer months to go cruising and the winter months to go visiting (neat, eh, summer in the UK and UK winter/Australian summer in, yes, Australia).

Free Time, the steel one, is berthed in Ripon, North Yorkshire. Now this is the most northern point of the connected inland waterway system, but still 100 miles from our home in Cumbria. We planned to exit our Ripon Marina, do a "left hand down a bit" and continue our merry way down to London. The exciting bit would be to sail under Tower Bridge and past the

Houses of Parliament and then return, by a different route, back to Ripon.

I relied heavily on the two main canal guides, *Pearson's Canal Companion* and *Nicholson's Waterways Guide*, to work out where I was going. There are choices as to whether it is "left hand down a bit" or, indeed, "right hand down a bit". Luckily they are few and far between (well, it may only be a few miles apart, but at our sedate speed of a maximum of 3 knots that usually give us a day or two to make the decision of which one it will be, so a canal guide is a good idea). It does also have the added bonus of telling you where the nearest pub is. I cunningly supplemented this information with a GPS, so it was not often we got caught out.

To keep in touch with the family, I undertook to write a daily journal and to email it to family members on a weekly basis. This journal is a contemporaneous record of our journey.

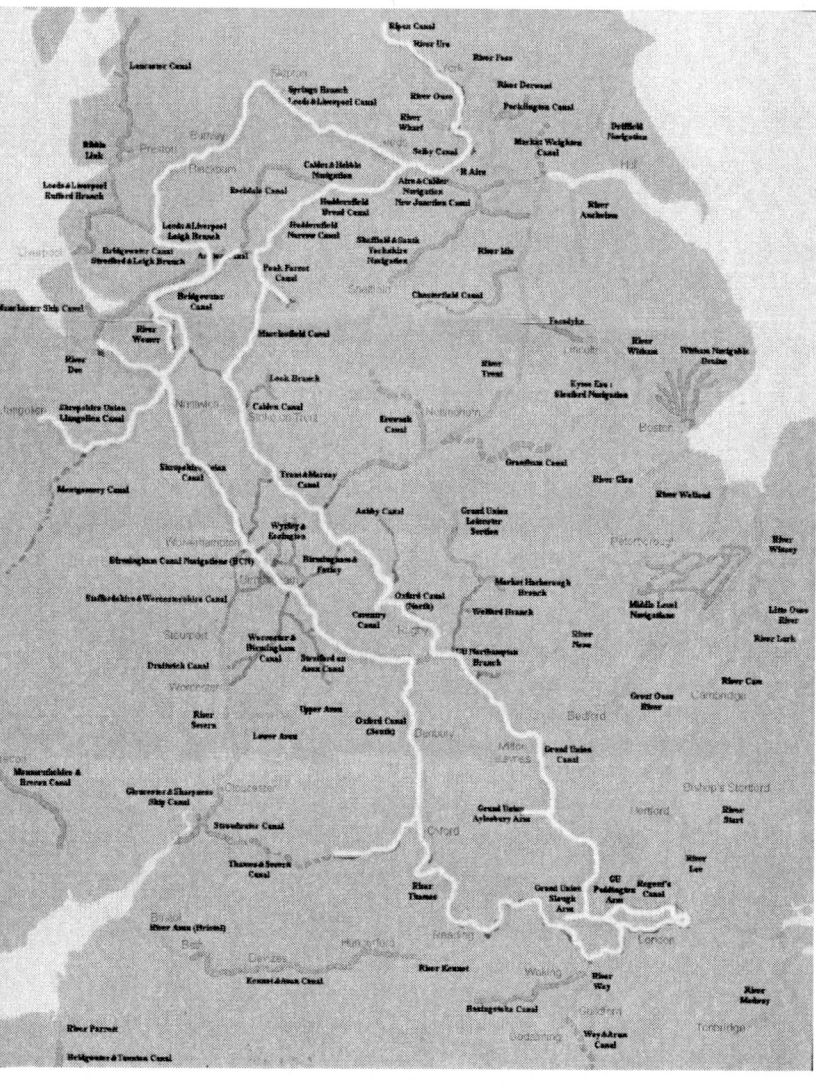

W/c Monday 10th April 2006

Free Time

Monday

The summer cruise of the grey nomads begins on a beautiful sunny spring day. It took forever to pack everything into the car, and my poor wife, Pam, has been cleaning the house for three days as our next-door neighbours, Bruce, Julia and their gorgeous children, the twins and little Adam, are moving into our house for a couple of months whilst they get their extension built. It is strange how opportunities present themselves. By coincidence we have established neighbours as house sitters, and they have convenient accommodation and can literally oversee their building work (presumably this will ensure there is no slacking by the builders). This is definitely one of those rare events, a win win situation. I must stop this management speak now I have retired. On the drive over from Cumbria to Yorkshire we have an excellent late lunch at a farm shop near Penrith, one of the benefits of foot-and-mouth forcing farmers to diversify five years ago. We arrive with all our gear at Ripon Marina early evening. The evening is spent with general unpacking and tidying up the boat. We will go and buy provisions tomorrow.

View from *Free Time's* berth

Tuesday

We spend the day pottering and buying enough provisions to last for a few days. Ripon town centre is a half-hour walk, which fits in well with one of Pam's retirement resolutions: walk at least three miles a day. Unfortunately another of her resolutions is no booze until after five o'clock (in the evening, that is, not the morning).

Ripon Cathedral

Wednesday

This was my day of a BIG adventure. I had to take our car home to Cumbria for the summer. No problem. Up at dawn to drive over (leaving Pam in bed…), stopped at Scotch Corner at our favourite lorry drivers' roadside café for a cup of tea and a fried egg roll (must stop being so predictable in retirement), and then home for eleven o'clock. As our son, Garry, says, "I'm not keen on public transport", but needs must. Despite planning to catch a bus from home to the town of Cockermouth, another bus from Cockermouth to Carlisle, train from Carlisle to Leeds and bus from Leeds, to Ripon, our neighbour, Bruce, insisted on giving me a lift to Carlisle, eliminating the need for the first two buses. Actually, I quite enjoyed the adventure even if it did take 10 hours. I borrowed Pam's MP3 player and played Kaiser Chiefs, Coldplay, Eurythmics, Shakira and Sugababes quietly headbanging away to the consternation of my fellow passengers.

Pam spent the day with a friend who came up from Harrogate for the day. Her sister and husband, Ann and John, and their blind dog (or is it dog for the blind?), Greg, joined us in the evening. They will stay a few days with us for the start of our five-month cruise.

Greg making himself at home

Thursday

This is the real start of our summer cruise. We left Ripon mid-morning (civilised start time). There was a very sharp blind corner exiting the marina. This gave us an early opportunity for trying out our walkie-talkies. I sent Pam down to the sharp end (front of the boat) with one walkie-talkie. The theory is that if another boat is around the corner, she can see it from the bow and radio back to the unsighted helmsman at the stern some fifty feet away. Anyway, no boat came so we have yet to find out whether Pam has mastered the technology or not. The weather was bright, sunny but very windy. This led to "interesting" helming of *Free Time,* particularly at locks. We cruised for a couple of hours and stopped at Boroughbridge. We lunched on board and then walked into town and along the river. Dinner was a take-away from the Indian restaurant this evening as we didn't want to leave Greg on his own (what a pampered dog).

Sharp corner at Ripon Marina

Friday

We woke up to a bright sunny morning with the wind dying down a little. We pottered around in the morning with a walk into Boroughbridge to provision up for the day. We set off at eleven o'clock (again) for the three-hour run down to Linton-on Ouse. This section is river and is very pretty indeed. This is a fairly remote part of the river with only a small pub for company (is there a theme here?). We had a brisk walk into the village and back (Greg loved it) and the main decision tonight is whether to have fish and chip special in the pub at £3.50 a head, or eat on the boat and go for a pint. We will probably go for the latter as Greg might not be welcome in the restaurant section. I spent the early evening drinking beer in the sun and polishing my brasses!

The boys in charge

Saturday

We had a relatively early start (well, half past nine) on an overcast morning. However, the wind had vanished which made everything OK. There was an uneventful trip of nine miles down to York. I spotted two kingfishers on the riverbank. John reckons they are the UK's parrots. We moored up in the middle of York, which is a very busy town with lots of one-way roads. We dispatched John by bus to pick up his car, which he had left at Ripon. The plan was for him to return to the boat and pick up Ann, Greg and associated luggage as they are returning home today. We weren't sure he would be able to find the way down to the river through the tangle of roads in and about York. However I had a brainwave. I marked the boat as a waypoint on my portable GPS, gave it to John and he had a nice lady's voice directions to take him back to exactly the right spot. Now he wants one too. Pam and I waved goodbye to the three of them. We shall miss them, especially Greg. We went off to the cinema to see Tommy Lee Jones' new film, *The Three Burials of Melquiades Estrada*. It is very good and to be recommended.

Very old York Abbey

Sunday

Pam and I spent the day pottering around York. I spent an hour at a WiFi hotspot in McDonalds (actually it was an upmarket McCafé and very good). The sun was shining from time to time and the temperature was too warm for a jacket, but just a little chilly for only a jumper. This exercised our minds each time we go went a walk. We walked around the walls which surround the city of York. I am sure we were well over our daily minimum of three miles a day. We had little light very late lunch and spent the evening at the theatre watching *Broadway Musical*.

York Minster

This completes our first week's journal. More thrilling tales next week.

W/c Monday 17th April 2006

Free Time

Monday

We pottered around York in the morning. The weather was very sunny, but also very windy. After buying provisions for the next few days and yet another outfit for Pam, we set off after lunch. We had pre-booked our passage on the tidal stretch of the River Ouse from Nayburn to Selby for Tuesday at half past eleven. Having sold our coastal sailing yacht to take up the softer option of inland waterway cruising, I thought I had given up having to worry about tide times! En route we fired up the washing machine, which worked a treat. It uses electricity generated by the engine; isn't science clever? We moored up at the tidal lock in a very pleasant and rural spot, and then went for our daily walk across the fields into the village of Nayburn. The village consists of typical pretty red brick houses and cottages – very picturesque. I went wood gathering in the surrounding woods. We had dinner on the boat, sat around our log fire and watched television tonight.

Bishopthorpe Palace

Tuesday

We had a late start as we were booked to go through the tidal lock at half past eleven. We set off, according to plan accompanied by a converted fishing vessel and a broad beam canal cruiser. The river from Nayburn to Selby is tidal with up to 4 knots of current. As our top speed is 4.5 knots, this can make manoeuvring interesting to say the least. This fourteen-mile stretch was pleasant and, in the latter stages, fast as the tide was behind us pushing *Free Time* towards Selby. Then came the interesting part. Selby lock is at right angles to the river. The technique is to go beyond the lock, do a 180 degree about turn (not easy in a 55ft narrowboat) and then approach the lock against the current. As you have to have the engine at high revs to make any headway at all, the 90 degree turn into the lock entrance is the nautical equivalent of a handbrake turn into a parking place. It did not help that the broad beam cruiser went into the lock ahead of *Free Time* as this narrowed the space to aim for from twenty feet to nine feet (*Free Time* is 7ft wide). We made it without touching either the lock wall or the cruiser!

After a visit to the chandlers in Selby, we continued onto a little hamlet called West Haddlesey, which is on the junction of Selby Canal and the River Aire. We travelled nineteen miles today. We took our evening constitutional in a glorious evening.

Tight squeeze at Haddlesey

Free Time **arrived last!**

Wednesday

The rain that had been forecast arrived overnight. We had a lazy morning until it stopped raining and set off at eleven o'clock. The day brightened up and became very sunny, if a little cold. The cold is no problem; the wood burning stove keeps the inside of the boat warm and snug. Today's trip was a combination of rivers and broad canals. There were some large commercial craft on the broad waterways. The scenery was a strange mixture of remote countryside and industrial landscapes. We arrived at Castleford by late afternoon. Pam went off to do some shopping whilst I pottered doing odd jobs on the boat (including unblocking the shower outlet pump). Castleford canalside is not overly attractive, so we pushed on to Lemonoyd marina, arriving mid-evening. This was a good move; it is pleasant, well kept, rural and really idyllic. We had lemon sole and salad for dinner on the boat and changed the curtain fittings (how domestic is that?). This was another big mileage day, with eighteen miles covered.

Queue for the lock

Thursday

We set off after breakfast for the short trip into Leeds city centre (seven miles and seven huge mechanised locks). The approaches are through mile after mile of derelict industrial wastelands (historians and canal buffs call it "industrial heritage"). However, despite the lack of scenic appeal, the wildlife along this part of the canal is abundant and varied, so someone must be getting it right. We moored up right in the city centre. It was a little too early in the season for the basin to be busy, but I believe in summer this is a very popular mooring. We wandered around Leeds the afternoon. I failed miserably in getting a WiFi connection. There were plenty of networks, but somehow I screwed up the setting on my laptop. I think I will have to pay someone to sort it out for me. I wrote up various journals and then this evening had pasta at a nice little Italian we know.

Thwaite Mill, Leeds

Friday

We left Leeds at nine o'clock in a slight drizzle. Two locks later we discovered that some silly sod had left a windlass at the previous lock (me!). Pam walked back and surprisingly it was still there. The weather steadily improved. Quite quickly we were out of the Leeds suburbs into pretty countryside. However, we were advised by some British Waterways lock-keepers that it was what they called "bandit country". The local yobs come down from the three housing estates just over the hill (out of sight) and generally harass boaters. However, apparently they don't get up until lunch-time, so a passage in the morning was no problem. We moored at Rodley mid-afternoon and had a late lunch. Rodley is a small Yorkshire village which took all of twenty minutes to walk round. We spent the afternoon in glorious sunshine. Pam re-varnished some of the wood and I touched up some of the paintwork where we had banged against a lock wall. I spent the early evening with my favourite pastime, drinking beer in the sun and polishing my brasses! We had fish and chips from the highly recommended local chip shop. The secret is in using dripping as frying fat; none of this vegetable oil rubbish.

All sorts of craft on the canal

Saturday

We were tired last night, so did not wake up until nine o'clock. We set off at ten o'clock in slightly misty weather, but a hot sunny day was forecast. The only issue of the day was a double lock staircase which gave us a few problems. One of our fenders fell off, so had to be fished out, not without some difficulty. A combination of stiff paddle gear, obstructions in the underwater gates and the previous boat leaving a paddle only half closed all caused quite a lot of delay. Oh yes, there was also a sight operator error, but we will not dwell on that! The next lock was a triple staircase. No problem; we breezed through that one. We moored up at a single mooring at Shipley. There is a sign which says it is a 24-hour mooring, but not to moor if the waterbus is due. However, there was no sign to say when the waterbus was due. We moored long enough to have a late lunch, do a bit of shopping at the nearby Aldi (all you can fill into a shopping trolley and you get change from a fiver) and a bit of WiFi-ing (I know, there is no such word) at the adjacent McDonalds. Observant readers amongst you will have noted that I couldn't get the WiFi to work in Leeds and threatened to actually pay someone to sort it out. Anyway, I got it to work after a lot of effort (but without paying anyone, mainly because there was no one around to pay). That was the good news; the bad news is I have no idea what I did, so when it happens again I am back to square one. In fear of an impending waterbus, we moved along to the next set of moorings. These are very upmarket, but surprisingly there are no other boats around. I'm not sure why, but we decided to set a precedent and stay overnight. We had a wander around Shipley and walked out to Saltaire, which is very impressive. There was no TV reception at the mooring, so we watched an Alfred Hitchcock DVD, *The Man Who Knew Too Much*.

Saltaire Church

Sunday

It was early start for me at eight o'clock, although Pam was still in bed. We travelled all of one mile and moored up in Saltaire in glorious sunshine. Saltaire is a model Victorian village founded by Sir Titus Salt for his woollen mill workers. Apparently, he made his money by being the first to formulate dyeing techniques for alpaca wool. He believed his workers deserved decent living conditions (this was in the mid-1800s), so he built good standard housing, church, library, hospital, etc. He also believed that the workers should have no booze, so there is no pub – not that he was teetotal himself, quite the reverse.

Obviously there is one rule for those that have and another for those that have not; no change there then. We spent a very pleasant day wandering around the self-guided tour of Saltaire, visiting the David Hockney exhibition (Pam wanted one for the dining room, I wouldn't give any houseroom!) and then walking across the River Aire to the tramway to take you to the top of Shipley Glen. The Victorian cable-car is very ramshackle, but great fun. It only operated at weekends, run by enthusiasts, and only cost 80p return. We moved *Free Time* another half-mile into a wooded glade. We had gin and tonics in the sun before walking back into Saltaire for a dinner of tapas (Pam wanted to practise her Spanish but found the waiter was pure Bradford) and caramelised bread and butter pudding with Anglais sauce which you would kill for. We were both a little red from the sun, but it was a good day all round.

This completes our second week's journal and we were not going stir-crazy (yet).

W/c Monday 24th April 2006

Free Time

Monday

We had another leisurely start this morning. It was a little chilly, so off I went gathering fuel from the surrounding woods. Not much is needed; half a poly bag will warm the cabin for a few hours until the day warms up around eleven o'clock. We went through a double staircase and then arrived at Bingley (a romantic name, isn't it?). We wandered into town for a little shopping. The name befits the town, which is downtrodden and a little shabby. The textile mills are now gone, bowing to the superior efficiency, or is it the lower wage cost, of the Far East? Thermal wear manufacturers Damart are hanging on, along with the other main employer, the Bradford and Bingley Building Society. Pam went off to buy provisions whilst I went to the

Wetherspoons pub for a pint and a WiFi (am I becoming a WiFi bore?). Anyway, I got a fast connection and sent off last week's journal to everyone. We set off again and immediately went through a triple staircase lock, closely followed by the famous Bingley Five Rise staircase. This is one of the waterway's wonders. Built in 1774, it changes the level of the canal by some sixty giddy feet, an exhilarating experience. After drinks on the boat we attended a Bingley Gilbert & Sullivan Society performance of *The Mikado* in the evening, and very good it was. A case of G&T followed by G&S. A doubling of yesterday's mileage was achieved today, two miles in three hours. Now is that relaxed or not?

Bingley Five Rise Staircase

Tuesday

A grey morning, but we did not let this dampen our spirits. After a washdown (both the boat and ourselves) we set off to match yesterday's mileage of two miles. This time we stopped at Riddlesden, which is effectively a suburb of Keighley. We visited a strange little chandler going by the name Puffer Parts. It is run by a Scot who looks like he just stepped off a West Coast puffer. It may not have been *The Vital Spark*, but he certainly looked like Para Handy. We walked into Keighley, some 2 miles away. En route, we had lunch at a Toby Inn, with a full carvery for a very modest cost which attracted lots of old age pensioners to the pub. Hopefully we did not blend in! Keighley is a pleasant town which seems to have successfully shaken off the textile industry decline. It has a number of handsome civic buildings as well as new shopping centres. The Brontë sisters did their shopping here having walked the four miles from Haworth. There and back eight miles come winter and summer puts our lowly two miles into perspective. We took a bus back to the boat for an afternoon of pottering and reading the papers in the sun before walking back into Keighley in the evening to attend a performance of Agatha Christie's *Love from a Stranger* at the Keighley Playhouse. The Playhouse is very quaint; at the interval we were served tea and biscuits at our seats from a tray in willow-pattern china teacups. Having walked more than our three miles a day quota, we took a bus back to the boat.

East Riddlesden Hall

Wednesday

Another grey morning, but once again the forecast was that the sun would burn off the cloud in the afternoon. No locks today again, but more than a few swing bridges in our five-mile sprint, stopping at the small town of Silsden. Our wander around Silsden did not take long, but it is quite pretty in an austere sort of way. It has a boatyard which acts as a holiday cruise hire centre, as well as a corn mill which dates from 1677. After getting a haircut, there was more polishing this afternoon and generally watching the world go by.

Silsden wildlife

Thursday

This was canal cruising at its finest. The weather is gloriously sunny and this nineteen-mile stretch of canal does not have any locks, only numerous swing-bridges which have to be opened at regular intervals, mainly by me as some of them are quite stiff. The canal hugs the contours of the hillsides, making for very picturesque scenes, especially cruising through woods and looking down at the valley below. Swans are nesting at this time of year. They can be very aggressive, defending their territory and in particular their nests from all intruders, including 55ft boats. They are definitely not to be messed with. We arrived early afternoon at Skipton, the self styled capital of the Yorkshire Dales. It was very busy with boats as there was a waterways festival over the bank holiday weekend. We had to moor slightly out of Skipton and walk back into town. It is a fine stone town with a good number of small (and big) shops, as well as a very pretty walk along the river and up to Skipton castle. This walk aptly starts at Stainforth's Celebrated Pie Establishment. We shall certainly be celebrating there tomorrow when we stock up with provisions. Having done our three miles walking, and had our evening gin and tonics (it was after five o'clock) we went off to the award winning Bizzie Lizzies fish and chip shop for a fish supper. This is the life...

Swan seeing off *Free Time*

Friday

We are staying in Skipton for a few days so no cruising today. Since retiring, I am constantly amazed at our ability to potter and while away time; walking into town, shopping a little, paper reading, polishing brasses, contemplating navels... There was increasing activity as some more very bright and shiny boats arrive for the waterways festival tomorrow. We went off to the cinema in the evening. There were two attractions: the picture house and the film. The Plaza Cinema in Skipton is an original period cinema (what period I am not sure, but I would guess from the 1930s; it still has an organ at the base of the screen which presumably is a throwback to the silent movies which were phased out in the late 1920s). The main feature (in fact the only feature – no multiplex here) was *The White Countess* by Merchant Ivory. This is one of their typical productions, a lavish, atmospheric, period drama. Based in Shanghai in the 1930s, it is basically a love story with a political backdrop. It is what Pam calls a woman's film, but it certainly held my attention.

Pam at waterfall at Skipton Castle

Saturday

We wandered into Skipton in the morning to watch the waterways festival. The day was sunny, and the start of the three-day festival seems to be going well. I looked at the doilies, the brightly painted canal ware, the Rosie and Jim dolls, and started to smile and drool not a little. Pam decided that enough was enough and dragged me away. So we set off at lunch-time for our next five miles of delightful canal cruising; destination Gargrave.

Skipton Waterways Festival

Gargrave is a largish village: very pretty with a few shops, three pubs and the ubiquitous Indian take away aptly named Bollywood Cottage. We were slightly over budget after the fleshpots of Skipton, so we ate in tonight.

River at Gargrave

Sunday

We woke to a warm, sunny day. On came the shorts and out came the knees; the first time this year, but hopefully not the last. Today's cruise consisted of three locks in quick succession, a circumnavigation (almost) of a number of hills as we snaked lovingly around each hill's contours, a sharp blast of six very pretty locks, and another flat bit culminating in the final three locks before mooring up at a tiny village called Salterforth. We have got into a bit of a routine. Pam does an imitation of the Idle Women from WWII and steers *Free Time* serenely into and out of the narrow locks, whilst I dash around like a mad thing opening lock gates, wrestling with ground paddles and generally working up a lather. We did a momentous ten miles today. We rewarded ourselves by a trip to the pub this evening for a few glasses of wine and a "home-made" bar meal. The Anchor Inn dates from 1655 and reputedly has stalactites in the cellar (apparently they can be viewed by appointment with the landlord). We were back in *Free Time* by nine o'clock, in time to watch an Agatha Christie mystery on the television (co-incidentally on ITV, which is the only channel we can get reception for this evening). Here ended another week and also the month. So far, no regrets...

Odd double bridge

This completes our third week's journal and we are not arguing (yet).

W/c Monday 1ˢᵗ May 2006

Free Time

Monday

What a difference a day makes. After the hot sunshine of yesterday, we woke to a wet, windy and cold morning. We had a long way to go, so appropriately set off at eight o'clock (well I did; Pam stayed below in the warmth). After an hour we arrived at the mile-long Foulridge Tunnel. It is famous in canal circles because in 1912 a cow, aptly named Buttercup, fell into the canal at the entrance of the tunnel. Even although this was before the days of mad cow disease, Buttercup was not too bright as she opted to swim into and along the tunnel instead of clambering out where she fell in. Now this caused a bit of commotion as there was not enough room for a narrowboat and a cow to pass in the confines of the tunnel. Buttercup eventually arrived exhausted at the other end of the tunnel, having swum the full mile length in pitch dark, before being rescued and revived with brandy. She lived to be milked another day. Shortly after Foulridge Tunnel we arrived at Barrowfield locks; all seven of them. The windy conditions made for hard work. The scenery took a turn for the worse as we cruised through a lot of urban and industrial decay in the towns of Barrowford, Nelson, Brierfield and Burnley, which ran into each other with no discernable boundaries. We had passed from the glorious Yorkshire Dales to the northern declining mill towns of Lancashire. The afternoon brightened somewhat, but there was still a strong cold wind. There was nowhere appealing to stop, so we ploughed on until we got to our overnight mooring at Hapton, a relatively pleasant grey little village with regular streets of terraced houses and three irregular public houses.

Spring Bank Holiday Monday in the UK

Tuesday

The forecast was not great for the day with wet and windy weather due in the afternoon/evening. With this in mind we set off promptly at nine o'clock to cover the eight miles to Rishton, which is on the outskirts of Blackburn. The canal crossed rural and agricultural countryside. There was quite a lot of weed, which seems to float loose and then joins forces with its mates to ambush an unsuspecting boat, usually at narrow bits of the canal. This inevitably slows progress and sometimes necessitates a visit to the weed hatch to free the propeller. Still, the canal was much improved on the urbanisation gone wrong from the previous day. The canal and the M65 motorway share the valley. Surprisingly we saw a roe deer on the tract of land between the canal and the motorway. It didn't look happy as it ran through the open countryside, but it did look cute. We arrived at Rishton at lunchtime. Rishton is another grey Lancashire "tillage" (well, it is too small for a town and too big for a village). The shops are uninspiring, but it does sport a small modern library. I had not been able to get a WiFi hotspot, for a few days so, anxious to please the readers of this journal, I made enquiries about whether I could use the library's computer. No problem; I copied last week's journal onto a memory stick, plugged it in to their computer and Hotmailed it off. They would not accept any payment. Nice people in Rishton… salt of the earth.

Rishton Church

Wednesday

What a glorious day... the forecast was hot and sunny, and it was. Another early start (yes, you guessed it: me on the tiller and Pam in bed). We followed a quite pleasant bit of the canal until we reached the outskirts of Blackburn. This proud Lancashire town has seen better days, but there are signs of regeneration, with some of the magnificent old mills being used for other purposes such as housing or retail outlets. In the middle of Blackburn are six locks in close proximity. We had not seen another boat moving for a couple of days, so undaunted we once again tackled the series of locks on our own. After Blackburn we cruised into attractive countryside with affluent farms and houses (there were lots of horses in evidence and, I think, we are in Cheshire, famous for "footballers' wives"). About lunch-time we arrived at our destination of Riley Green. This consists of a pub with very good moorings for customers. We walked into the hamlet, about half a mile away. There was nothing of note so we walked back. The mooring is very pretty. We pottered in the afternoon in the sunshine doing a bit of polishing and having the odd gin and tonic. We felt obliged to have dinner in the pub as they were providing the moorings. Another day had flown by.

Sporting shorts in Blackburn

(incidentally I am refilling *Free Time* with water)

Thursday

The forecast was for a very hot sunny day. Once again it did not look at all promising when we set off, but by eleven o'clock, Pam was looking for the suntan lotion. Again the canal was rural and pretty. We arrived at Johnson's Hillock Locks about eleven o'clock. These are a series of seven locks. The locks are well maintained and easy to operate in a beautiful rural setting. We stopped at Botany Bay (I think this may be the original rather than the upstarts in Australia). There is a large mill converted into a themed retail park. We moored up and went for a wander. We were very upset to find we were actually charged to get in; the cheek of asking us for money for the privilege of spending more money. Anyway, they got the former but we steadfastly refused to contribute to the latter. After lunch on the boat we cruised for another hour and moored up at Adlington. This is yet another tillage (remember, too large for a village but not big enough for a town). It boasts no less than five pubs, a bank (Royal Bank of Scotland, no less) and a number of nondescript shops, including a Co-op. We did a little shopping for provisions, went to the pub for a pint of Old Spectacled Hen, a Jennings brand, which is our local brewer at home, and back to the boat to chill over a gin and tonic. Whilst cruising through the urban sprawls of Burnley and Blackburn, we were treated to the gentle wafting of curry spices most of the way from what was no doubt Asian grannies cooking up dinners for the families. This must have imprinted a subliminal message in my brain as, unusually, I had an insatiable craving for a curry. Off we went to the Sharju which specialises in Raj Cuisine (whatever that means). It is in a converted church, in Church Street. You couldn't make it up, could you? The curry, surroundings and service were excellent, although perhaps our breaths were not exactly mint fresh.

The Sharju Indian restaurant

Friday

It was a very early start for me at six o'clock. This was the day we had to do the Wigan flight of locks, all twenty-three of them. We had arranged to meet another boat, *Hakuna Matata*, at the first lock gate at nine o'clock, so had to set off that early to get there on time. Two boats instead of one means half the work. Even better, they had asked a couple of friends to join them for the day, so it was actually a third of the work. Now then, where does the name *Hakuna Matata* come from? The first person to e-mail me with the answer will be mentioned in despatches no less (I already know because I asked...). The Wigan flight of locks consists of twenty-three locks (did I mention that before?), all tightly packed. It is hard work and I defy anyone to actually keep count as they do one lock after another. After the first four or five, they become a homogeneous blur. Three and a bit hours later, we emerged at the bottom of the flight, tired, grubby, red from the sun, but happy. The canal now enters a phase of traversing one nature reserve after another. This used to be a big coal mining area. The whole area is prone to subsidence and as such no other use can be found for the land, hence they are converted to nature reserves, each sporting their very own "flash". "Flash" is the name given to a lake formed by a subsidence of land subsequently filling with water. Whatever the origin, it is now quite pretty and a haven for birds. Another hour found us at Dover – Cheshire, not Kent. This is a village (note, village, not tillage). It has one pub by the canal and that is about it. We were quite tired so are happy for a little walk (we walked well over three miles on the Wigan flight) and a potter in the afternoon sun. We had a quiet evening with the television and an early night.

Hakuna Matata and *Free Time* breasted up at Wigan flight

Saturday

We woke to another hot sunny morning. A couple of months ago the huge counterweights on a lift bridge at Plank Land suddenly fell off, much to the consternation of British Waterways (and indeed anyone who was unlucky enough to be around at the time). Anyway, it is still not fixed, so once a fortnight Bright Waterways organise a very large crane to come and physically lift the bridge. This only gives boaters a four hour window each fortnight to cross Plank Lane. It has an interesting effect of concertinaing the narrowboats. There were about thirty in each direction waiting to get through. It was quite a colourful sight, and not a little congested. We stopped for lunch at the ancient town of Worsley. The manor of Worsley is first mentioned in 1195. Coal has been mined here since the 14th century. There are some forty-six miles of tunnels, shafts and general black holes, all dug out by hand (well I guess a few spades and pick axes were also involved). This is reported to be the birthplace of the canal system. The Duke of Bridgewater started building the canal in 1759 to transport the coal from his mines to the industrial town of Manchester. I know a great Italian restaurant in Worsley, so had promised Pam we would have lunch there. Unfortunately, for some reason it was closed, so we had to settle for a mediocre pub lunch at the Brewers Fayre next door. We continued after lunch to the centre of Manchester and moored up about five o'clock. After a brief wander around we found a new AMC sixteen-screen multiplex cinema. We decided to see *Mission Impossible 3*. This is a high tech, action film starring Tom Cruise: a bit of pap, but enjoyable pap.

Worsley – iron deposits colour the water here

Sunday

Sunday was spent pottering around Manchester city centre. Manchester is a fine city with many magnificent Victorian buildings. I also detect a change of atmosphere in Manchester; it is becoming more of a café society, although the hard drinking, clubbing reputation is still in evidence. The IRA bombing of some ten-plus years ago perversely may have had a positive effect, with the extensive rebuilding being done in a more sympathetic manner than the 1960s shopping arcades they have replaced. About 100 yards from our mooring, there was a small collection of trailers and a bus or two. Being nosey, I walked around this morning to discover it was in fact a mobile kitchen for a film/TV set. Pam and I were having coffee in a little arcade in the centre of town this morning to find we were in the middle of a film shoot. It was all very interesting. (Now I know why film/TV drama is so expensive. There seemed to be zillions of people just hanging around as they did take after take. No doubt they are all being paid a lot for the privilege.) Apparently, they were shooting a detective series based in Manchester for ITV. Pam recognised Ray Winstone, but we have no idea who else is in it, or indeed what it is called. No doubt we will be viewing the TV listings avidly from now on in the hope, nay anticipation, that we will be making a guest appearance (royalty cheque is in the post). Despite our being in a city centre, I had great difficulty in locating a BT Openzone hotspot. There are lots of other service providers in evidence, but I have to pay for them at an average of £4 per half-hour, and I am too mean for that. Plan B swung into action. I phoned our son Garry and asked him to look up BT Openzone hotspots in our area on the web (preferably pubs rather than McDonalds). He duly rang back with a whole list of them. This week's journal was e-mailed off this evening from The George Hotel, 121 Liverpool Road, courtesy of Garry. We now only had to decide where to eat tonight. The choice is between a Greek tapas bar called Demitri's (contradiction, I know) or a noodles/sushi bar which always looks busy, so we surmise it must be good.

Manchester Town Hall

This completes our fourth week's journal. We have travelled 191 miles, done 107 locks, swung open 41 bridges and cruised for 88 hours so far.

W/c Monday 8th May 2006

Free Time

Monday

We woke up to typical Manchester weather (allegedly), overcast and drizzly. Pam's old boss (old in the sense that she used to be her boss; no aspersions about age are implied or otherwise), Vera of Allison's Chemist fame, and hubbie, Allan, joined us at ten o'clock. Their son, David, lives in Stockton Heath, some nineteen miles away. They were visiting David, and took a taxi out to Manchester to be crew for the day. We had some coffee and then set off towards Stockton Heath. It took us about two hours to get out of the suburbs of Manchester, only to reach the suburbs of Sale. Unlike the urban decay of the Lancashire towns last week, there is a lot of regeneration in Manchester aptly called Urban Splash. At about half past eleven, Pam suggested that Vera would like a white wine. I asked what had happened to the five o'clock rule, only to be given that look which says "just do it". Allan very quickly took to helming, like a proverbial duck to water, which let me have the time to open the various bottles of wine. After a few glasses, Allan let slip that it was their 35th wedding anniversary, a good excuse to open a bottle of Moet & Chandon which I just happened to have chilling in the fridge. We had a leisurely lunch on board at Dunham Town, which is a tiny hamlet, and not even big enough to be a tillage. All trip we had a running commentary from Allan, who is a farmer, on the state of the various crops in the surrounding fields, and the demise of the cows quietly chewing the cud. At lunch we had the entertainment of a solitary poor farmhand, who had the misfortune to be repairing a wire fence just where we were moored up. It was just as well he could not hear Allan's somewhat caustic comments on the efficiency of his work. The canal from Sale, through Lymm and onto Stockton Heath is quite pretty with wooded glades and prosperous canalside housing. We arrived at Stockton Heath at five o'clock (only seven hours back for Vera and Allan after their half-hour taxi journey to meet us). We all went out for a meal at a local restaurant, the Loch Fyne Oyster Bar no less, and jolly fine it was. Fish all round.

The girls concentrating

Tuesday

There was heavy rain during the night, but it was bright and sunny by the time we surfaced. We walked into Stockton Heath. It is a little up-market town. The number of restaurants is quite amazing. There are more per square yard than I have ever seen before. Obviously the Stockton Heathonians don't possess kitchens in their homes; they just eat out each and every meal to support the local eateries. Pam bought some more plants for her flower tubs, and off we set. The countryside really is very pleasant, although everything always looks better in the sun. At

Preston Brook we took a detour along the Runcorn arm of the Bridgewater Canal. Now, I know Runcorn well as it is not far from the chemical plant I used to work at in Widnes. I know it is not exactly a prime tourist destination, but I had heard that the canal route was quite attractive. Indeed it is. The canal meanders through bluebell woods, passes priories and parks, and in general is a real gem of a waterway. It is five miles long and only the last mile and a bit when we get into Runcorn leaves a little to be desired, but even Runcorn looks better from the water on a sunny day. We stopped for lunch in one of the bluebell woods beside Norton Priory: a truly idyllic spot. Detour over, we continued on the Bridgewater Canal onto the Trent and Mersey Canal. The actual demarcation between these two canals takes place in the 1,239 yard Preston Brook tunnel. There may have been a notice or a mark on the wall, but it was far too dark to tell. We had more meandering in a rural setting before mooring up for the evening in open country. We wandered down to a pub on the River Weaver for our G & Ts and back to the boat in time for *The Archers*. This has been yet another sun-kissed day.

Rape seed crop flowering

Wednesday

Yet another glorious day… the forecast was hot and sunny, and it was. Not far to go today, so we had a fairly leisurely start around nine o'clock. The Trent and Mersey canal is what is known as a narrow canal (the first we have been on this trip). It is definitely decidedly narrow in parts, but that makes for a more interesting trip. We only had four miles to go before reaching the Anderton Lift. However, the four miles included two tunnels, the Saltersford Tunnel at 424 yards and the Barnton Tunnel at 572 yards. These are relatively short and must be a cowpat walk for our esteemed Buttercup. However, there is no traffic control system in these tunnels. Although Saltersford is the shorter, it also has several bends in it, so there is no way of knowing whether a boat is already steaming in your direction. It is a case of "who dares wins". The Anderton Lift is indeed another of the wonders of the waterways (remember the Bingley five?). Built in 1875 by Sir Edward Leader-Williams, it consists of two caissons, each capable of lowering and lifting (at the same time…) two narrowboats some sixty feet between the canal above and the River Weaver below. It was quite exiting launching *Free Time* into fresh air, and then to be somewhat jerkily lowered down to the river. We only had a short journey on the River Weaver to reach Northwich. After scaling (or should it be de-scaling, as we descended sixty feet) the canal heights (literally and figuratively) we now got to the serious purpose of the day; finding a hairdresser for Pam. Having scoured the streets of Northwich, and consulted with the tourist information centre, we settled on a somewhat up-market salon called Phase One. The appointment was duly set for one o'clock tomorrow afternoon. It remains to be seen (and probably heard) whether or not it is up to scratch.

Anderton Lift

Thursday

The heat wave continued for yet another day. The morning was spent pottering around Northwich awaiting Pam's hair appointment in the afternoon. Northwich is a strange, but not unpleasant town. It has a large number of mock Tudor buildings, typical of the Cheshire plain. However, it also has a number of arcades and side streets which were obviously erected in the 1960s and 1970s (flat-roofed single story buildings); very strange. The River Weaver runs through the centre of Northwich, but for some reason the town has turned its back to the water. There is not a single café, pub, restaurant, or commercial building actually utilising the river-banks, which are quite attractive. This is an opportunity lost, but not by some housing developers, who have a number of pricey sites on the fringe of town. Pam went off for her hair appointment, and I went off to a WiFi pub with my laptop. Two hours later we met up and Pam was very pleased with her hair (see photograph overleaf); so was I, on two levels. Firstly, I liked it a lot, and secondly, I was very thankful that Pam liked it, otherwise I suspect there could have been a recurring theme in our conversation for a considerable time. We went to the cinema in the evening to see *Take the Lead*, starring Antonio Banderas. This is an urban tale about under-privileged New York kids learning respect and how to make life choices by learning ballroom dancing. My succinct critique is "tripe!"

Pam's new hairdo

Friday

There are not many locks on the River Weaver, but they are manned and have set times for going up and down. Therefore a trip needs a little planning, because if you miss a locking time this adds two hours waiting time and knocks the schedule to hell. The plan was to set off at a quarter to eight to be at the first lock for eight o'clock and be able to reach the second lock at nine o'clock. What actually happened was that we woke up at ten past eight and set off at a quarter past. We cleared the first lock at twenty-five to nine and radioed ahead to the next lock telling them we were on our way. We had *Free Time* belting along at six knots. Poor girl did not know what had hit her, but she made it with five minutes to spare. The next couple of hours were spent at a more leisurely pace, yet again in the sunshine. First we passed a heronry. These birds look majestic when you see them at the riverside fishing. However, up on top of a tree, trying to sit on an untidy haystack of a nest, they are a most incongruous sight. They look very silly indeed. Next we passed a salt mine (see photo below). Cheshire has been famous since Roman times for its vast quantities of salt deposits. I hadn't realised that they just dug bloody great holes and mined it like you would coal. Perhaps I will think twice about having this stuff on my chips. We reached the source of the River Weaver at Winsford Flash, did a U-turn and returned to the Anderton Lift. We deliberately went up river because it looked more interesting on the map. Whilst sharing the Anderton Lift with another narrowboat, you get chatting, as you do. The guy on the narrowboat was local and said he always goes down river as it is very much prettier than up river. By this time we were suspended thirty feet in the air. Don't you hate it when some smart Alec has just confirmed you have taken completely the wrong decision?

Salt Mine

Saturday

The long hot spell had finally broken. There was heavy rain overnight and the morning ushered in drizzle and showers with a significant drop in temperature. Were we downhearted? We were certainly not; we just donned the wet gear and got on with it. Very soon we came to Anderton Marina. It has an interesting little pump out vessel (for you non-nautical types, a pump out is the discharge of the boat's holding tank from the toilet. It is always a great topic of conversation when "boaties" get together.). Anyway, this little vessel is unusual insomuch as there is normally a fixed point on shore which you drive up to rather than have the pump out come to you. Whoever thought of this is very imaginative. He (or she) named the boat *Two Loos Lautrec*! We had quite a short cruise of half an hour, then we stopped at Marbury Country Park to try and get our three-mile walk in early. We spent a great hour and a half wandering through the woods. The bluebells were still magnificent, but obviously were on the wane. I took my binoculars for a walk hoping to spot my bogey bird, the lesser spotted woodpecker (it still is my bogey bird). We carried on to a pub at Broken Cross and had lunch there. It had a good WiFi signal, so I e-mailed a spreadsheet into my old company which they had asked me to do (see, I am indispensable after all). We continued in the afternoon to Middlewich and moored up for the night at about five o'clock. The ten miles, and one lock, for the day were delightful. The canal is narrow and twists and turns through narrow bridges, sharp turns in wooded areas and generally holds your interest every inch of the way. We were well pleased with the day, even if it did rain most of the time.

Two-Loos Lautrec

Sunday

We woke up to a fairly dull, overcast day. We set off early (well, for us), just after eight o'clock. It was a pleasant, but uneventful cruise through to Calverley, which is on the northward bit of the Shropshire Union Canal to Chester and Ellesmere Port. We stopped at Barbridge for lunch, and then continued around to Calverley, arriving early afternoon. We spent a bit of time sprucing up *Free Time* as some friends, John and Ros Mrozik, and Allan and Georgie Laing (Jo, their daughter also turned up), had arranged to meet us in the evening for drinks and dinner. After sinking a few G & Ts and a couple of bottles of champagne, we set off to the Dysart Arms for dinner, and excellent it was as well, a good day all round.

Alpacas in an adjoining field (amazing what you see in England's pleasant land)

Yet another week has come and gone (five weeks in all). The speed time is passing is very worrying (well, you have to worry about something…).

W/c Monday 15th May 2006

Free Time

Monday

Another Monday, and this time the rain had set in as though it meant it. It was the first time we have had rain virtually all day. We were on the Shropshire Union Canal at Carveley. The original plan was to go to the northern terminal of the canal at Ellesmere Port. However, we seemed to be caught in a series of venues (with times) with friends who were keen to tie up with us, so our itinerary was looking more than a little challenging. As we were committed to being at Beeston for a barbeque on Wednesday evening, the plan was to get up very early and set off towards Ellesmere Port at about six o'clock. A combination of bad weather and a hangover from the excesses of our previous evening brought about a rethink. Pam still needed to (her words, not mine) do some shopping for the Monaco Grand Prix at the end of the month, and the only town we would be going through before then was Chester. So we left at nine o'clock and arrived at Chester about five o'clock, give or take an hour or so for lunch. This canal is broad, which negates slightly the anticipation of what is around the next corner. It also has stretches of mile after mile of moored boats which slows down progress dramatically as we, of course, obey the unwritten rule of the canal: "slow down when passing moored boats". If you don't, you can be sure an irate boater will emerge from the bowels of his, or her, boat to give you an earful. The canal goes through open countryside which is not unpleasant. Shortly after we set off we saw a herd of twenty or thirty deer, grazing on the hillside. The ruins of the 13th century Beeston Castle on top of a massive rocky outcrop can be seen for miles around. It is very dramatic indeed. On the outskirts of Chester we descended five locks, each accompanied by wonderful lock-keepers' houses (the houses, that is, although I am sure the lock-keepers were also wonderful). Of course, there are no longer lock-keepers and these houses are now private dwellings. As they tend to be remote with, sometimes, no road access, I guess they are bought by somewhat eccentric people who in turn have a very definite, and entertaining, view of lifestyle and décor. In one of them, there was a serious menagerie of donkeys and a peacock. The donkeys don't move a lot, and the peacock just makes a lot of noise. We moored up for the evening in the centre of Chester, just under the city walls

Typical bluebell wood

Tuesday

Today was one for a "serious shop", as Pam puts it. It was quite a nice day as she went off, credit cards in hand. I pottered around Chester with the task of finding where the theatre is and what was on. As it transpired nothing was on, as they are on a two-day change-over of shows. This left only the cinema. As we are not in Chester on Wednesday or Thursday, we cannot attend the Silver Screen showing for persons of a certain age for £2.70 (including refreshments). It would have been *March of the Penguins,* which I quite fancy, but know that I would never be able to persuade Pam to join the golden oldies for an afternoon; just as well it is Tuesday, so no potential conflict. However, the good news is we can attend *Ice Age II*, which I have wanted to see for some time now, but Pam was always embarrassed about going as she thinks it is a kids' film. All the other films fell into three categories: a) we had seen them before, b) they got turkey reviews, and c) they started too late for me not to guarantee falling asleep half-way through. Chester is not dissimilar to York. It is an ancient walled city which has been both carefully preserved and also any development within the walls has been subject to strict planning permission. I am impressed. There are no less than three separate ghost walks leaving on a daily basis from the impressive Town Hall, which houses the Information Centre in one of its wings. The cathedral (see photo on the next page) is directly opposite the Town Hall. I also bought an outsize umbrella to replace my somewhat tatty golfing umbrella, which I managed to lose overboard a few days ago (they don't float). Pam arrived back for lunch on the boat without having bought anything. I can see her stress levels rising. Off she went again, leaving me to have a beer and read the paper (finished both Sudokus in the *Telegraph*). Pam eventually got back by late afternoon with even higher stress levels (but a lot of parcels). She has at least a million and one outfits but she is sure none of them are suitable for Monaco. I dragged her off for a walk around the city walls. This was great. You get all sorts of fantastic views down on a very old city. We went to the early evening showing of *Ice Age II*. This, too, was great. It was clever, funny and solved all the world's woes (I lied about the last bit). We picked up a fish and chip supper and washed it down with Irn-Bru; sophisticated or wot?

Chester Cathedral

Wednesday

The forecast was pretty diabolical; unseasonable rain and gale force winds were due mid-afternoon. With this in mind we set off relatively early (well, eight o'clock). We turned around at Chester and retraced our steps as far as Beeston, some eleven miles away. The day was overcast and threatening, but no rain...yet. The journey was quite uneventful, apart from encountering the menagerie at the horribly named "Chemical Lock". The donkeys were as static as ever, but the peacock was quite animated and came over to supervise our lock-opening technique, accompanied by its friend, a strutting cockerel which we managed to overlook when we passed on Monday. We arrived at Beeston at three o'clock and spent four hours pottering and reading the papers until we were picked up by a friend, John Mrozik, in the pouring rain. Undeterred, we duly had our barbeque, drank too much, watched the European Cup Final, and generally chewed the fat. When we got back to the boat, the rain had stopped and there was no wind. The forecast for tomorrow and the next few days say rain and wind.

Barbeque at the Mroziks

Thursday

We set off once again at eight o'clock to make the most of the day before the very windy weather came in again later. There were a large number of kingfishers around today. Strangely, I had not noticed any en route since Leeds. They are great little birds with their fluorescent turquoises and browns: a beautiful sight which always remain a day's highlight, no matter how many times you have seen them. After about three hours, we reached Barbridge junction again. This time we headed down the Shropshire Union Canal into uncharted territory. We took a sharp right hand turn into the Llangollen Canal and immediately climbed four locks. Llangollen Canal has a reputation of being one of the most scenic in the system. It is certainly narrow; you even have to lift the side fenders to fit in the first lock because it is so tight. The day's weather forecast proved to be remarkably accurate with sunshine and showers, but with an increasing wind strength. Llangollen Canal acts as a water feeder from Wales to the thirsty English. This is highly unusual for a canal, but it does mean that it is a little like cruising uphill against the noticeable current. This is particularly accentuated at bridge holes, which are not only narrow, but very shallow. It can make for slow going, but I guess we will fly through on the way back. The other peculiarity of the Llangollen Canal is that the locks are accompanied by by-washes which cut across the canal at right angles. A combination of the strong gusty wind, the current, the by-washes and the very narrow entrances to locks and bridges make interesting steering problems. We moored up a four o'clock at a little village called Wrensbury. It really is idyllic, although I could not find the proverbial duck pond mentioned in the guide books. We walked into the village centre to get provisions as we have only cans of baked beans left (although we did remember to replenish the gin whilst in Chester). There was only one small shop, so provisions are still limited. As we are having friends join us tomorrow, I guess we will have to take them to the pub for lunch. There is good TV reception here, so it was beans and toast and *Eastenders* tonight.

Wrensbury boat yard

Friday

We had a lazy morning as we were waiting on Vera, Carolyn and Jean (again of Allisons Chemist fame) to join us for the afternoon. The time just flew – by the time you get up, tidy the boat up, tidy yourself up, read the newspapers and dunk your biscuit in your coffee... the girls arrived bang on time at twelve-thirty. As we could not do any meaningful shopping for food at the aforementioned shop in Wrensbury, we went to the Dusty Miller pub on the canalside for eats. Lunch was very good, if a little slow. This is one of the drawbacks of freshly cooked food, but it was worth the wait. We eventually set off at two o'clock in quite a pleasant afternoon, if still a little windy. The afternoon cruising started immediately with a lift bridge and was followed by a succession of locks, ten in all. We think the visitors from Allisons enjoyed themselves. The decibel levels in the boat were certainly high all afternoon. The only incident was towards the end of the afternoon when we were going up a sequence of six locks close together and a boat coming down nipped in and filled a lock which we were about to enter (the technical term is "stealing one's water"). I was not happy and scowled a lot at them, but they seemed impervious to my black looks. I must practise more at being a Grumpy Old Man. We dropped the girls off at five o'clock at the top of the six-lock staircase at Grindley Brook, and they were picked up by a taxi to take them back to their car which they had left at Wrenbury. Pam and I continued for an hour to the Whitchurch arm of the canal. We had a light supper on board, listened to *The Archers*, and then walked into town about a mile away. Whitchurch is a fine market town famous for its cheeses and its clocks. It has a number of beautiful period houses in the town centre. It was originally a Roman settlement called Mediolanum. It has a striking 14th century church called St Alkmund's Church. It almost featured in the journal, but Pam reckoned that I was getting obsessed with photographing churches (and I had forgotten to take the camera).

Carolyn pretending she knows what she is doing

Saturday

The forecast overnight rain was late. So, unfortunately, we had rain in the morning instead. We wanted to get to Ellesmere for the evening, so we set off anyway. This stretch of the Llangollen Canal is particularly remote and an under-populated area, passing no villages (never mind a tillage). The habitat certainly seems to suit the birdlife. We were knee-deep with the little blighters. Robins were everywhere, sparrows would land on the boat, chaffinches would elbow each other off the branches, and goldfinches would squabble for fun. What a great ornithological paradise. We also passed right through the middle of Whixall Moss. This is a raised bog very rich in flora and fauna. It is also very rich in adders, being one of the most densely snake-infested swamps in the UK (or perhaps the only one). There is one swing bridge in the middle of the bog which has to be manually opened. Guess who stayed on the boat? The canal crosses over the border into Wales (no passport required), obviously doesn't like it very much, and crosses back into England. It then has second thoughts and tries Wales again, only to revert to its original instincts and scurries back into England. It is all very confusing. We arrived at Ellesmere by mid-afternoon, which is already heaving with boats. We shoehorned our way into the last space, and went off to explore town. The guide book says "Ellesmere is a small country town with no pretensions". I think this is the equivalent of estate agent speak for "dowdy and down at the heel". We did not like it, so spat out our dummies and left. We cruised for a couple of hours later than we planned, but the scenery was spectacular in the evening sun. Saturday is the change-over day for the many boat hire companies in this area. There is entertainment to be had as some of the crews have never been on a boat before. They are easily spotted as they lurch from canalside to canalside, occasionally just missing, occasionally bouncing off to be deflected into the path of oncoming traffic. The trick is to ensure you are not the oncoming traffic. We caught up with a hired boat which was doing some of the bouncing, but followed at a respectful distance. However, this boat in turn caught up with another hire boat which was being very cautious indeed. To be fair the bridges are narrow and have quite a head current; however, they were averaging about a knot and a half and there was no way to get past them. After a half hour of this, we gave up, tied up and went to the pub

Pam dodging the adders

Sunday

There are days when you just run out of superlatives to describe them. This was one of those days. The plan was to set off early to reach the terminus of the canal in Llangollen by early afternoon. The day was once again rainy in the morning (but at least there was no wind) with some brightening up in the afternoon. The scenery moved from England's rolling pastures to Welsh Mountains. However, the clever bit is that the canal remained at the same level. We crossed the border yet again into Welsh Wales. To cope with the dramatic Welsh scenery, the canal plunges into hillsides through tunnels, emerging to soar above valleys on aqueducts and then clings precariously around mountainsides. It is narrow, scary and wonderful. Luckily it was still quite early in the season, so the canal is not too busy. I should imagine there is complete chaos and not a few tempers frayed in mid-season as boats try to pass each other at impossible (or should it be impassable) corners. The climax is the world famous Pontcysllte Viaduct (OK, you may not have heard of it). Built in 1805, it spans the River Dee at 126ft above the valley and is 1,007 ft long. That is the easy bit. The difficult bit is that it has no side. There is the towpath, with a guard rail and the canal (all 7ft of it), then nothing; well, a tiny little bit of metal to keep the water in. You drive the boat over the aqueduct with absolutely nothing on one side of you apart from a 126ft fall: not at all good for my vertigo. The policy was one of eyes straight in front, don't look down, and pray. On the other side of the aqueduct is the small town of Trevor. From Trevor to Llangollen, about five miles, is a magically beautiful canal full of twists, turns, narrow bits, and strong currents, and it is a joy to navigate (is this all too gushing?). We arrived at Llangollen as planned and moored up. There is a charge of £5 a night, including electricity, so we had the lights and TV on all night to get our money's worth. The town is very pleasant, if a little touristy. I went to a bank cashpoint and was asked by the machine which language I wanted to deal in, Welsh or English. Foolhardily I chose Welsh and managed to get some cash (Bank of England banknotes). There were no WiFi connections anywhere along the Llangollen that I could find, but I will visit the library to try to get this week's journal off tomorrow. We will visit a little bistro tonight; methinks (Ceasars or The Corn Mill).

Steam Train in Llangollen

Another week has sped by. We need to be in Manchester next Thursday to fly out to Monaco, so next week's journal will in fact be the next fortnight's journal truncated into one week. I am sure avid readers will be disappointed not to have their thrilling weekly instalment from the grey nomads, but normal service will be resumed when we get back.

W/c Monday 22nd May 2006

Free Time

Monday

We walked into Llangollen in the morning to see if we could e-mail the journal from the library. Free internet access is available, but they will not allow use of a memory stick, so although we picked up our messages, we could not send the journal. Readers will just have to wait a little until a Plan B is thought out. We reversed yesterday's journey, and it was just as spectacular going the other way as well. The big difference was that we were going down current this time. The bridge holes and narrow, shallow bits against which we had to rev the engine to make any headway now acted as if we were corks in a bottle. We shot through these pinch spots with alacrity; it was a little disconcerting to bear down on various obstructions on the canal at such a rate of knots. We also made full use of the walkie-talkies. At blind, narrow stretches where two boats cannot pass, Pam walked ahead and radioed back when the way was clear. It saved getting rude surprises and worse, having to reverse back a few hundred yards or so; never an easy task even over a few yards. We made a slight detour up into the basin at Trevor to refuel at the boatyard there. It was packed with boats, so we threaded our way through impossibly narrow spaces as boats were stacked up three or four deep. After turning around, we elbowed our way as close to the fuel pump as we could get (four boats in the trot) and fill up with 100 litres. The cost of diesel has gone up to 55per litre (it was 49p less than a month ago). Once again we got behind a hire boat which was going painfully slowly weaving its way along the cut. This time Pam simply went down to the front of the *Free Time* and asked then to move over to allow us to pass. Yes, I was tailgating them, and yes, Pam was getting bolshie, although she did ask ever so nicely. We kept going until seven o'clock in the evening as we wanted to cover as many miles as we could – we have to be at Barbridge by lunch-time on Thursday. We happened to have reached Ellesmere by seven o'clock, so we moored on the outskirts of town and ate in.

Sheer drop from Pontcysyllte Aqueduct

Tuesday

Despite an "iffy" forecast, we awoke to a clear, bright sunny morning, although there had been heavy overnight rain. I got my chamois leather out and dried off *Free Time* before setting off with a light and righteous heart. It is amazing what a little pre-breakfast work does to your ego. We said farewell to Ellesmere (again) with no regrets. The canal's nature had changed again, reflecting the rolling pastures of Shropshire. There were not many wooded areas, but there were lots of narrow bridge holes and blind corners to keep one's interest. It is a irrefutable law of boating that you never meet oncoming boats on broad straight bits; it is always, but always, at blind corners or at narrow bridge holes or, most likely, at both together. Still, everyone was polite and in good humour apart from one brusque boater (and no, it wasn't me). We moored up again at Whitchurch for lunch and walked into the town in the afternoon. Pam went off shopping for bits and pieces and I went to the library clutching my memory stick. This time the library had free internet access and they let you upload files. I have no idea why different authorities have different policies, but you should now all have last week's journal. This was obviously Plan B. It was such a pleasant afternoon that we decided to push on a bit further than planned and descended the six locks at Grindley Brook (three of them are in a staircase). We were helped through by a gnarled looking and somewhat taciturn lock-keeper. It is our custom to give lock-keepers a bottle of beer if they help us through a lock. It was worth it to see the look of surprise and gracious gratitude from our lockie. I could have sworn he touched his forelock as he hurriedly secreted the beer bottle in his ample jacket. If he had a cap, I am sure he would have doffed it. At the bottom of the locks, we found a quiet and pretty mooring for the evening. Pam produced a risotto with just about everything in it (apart from the frozen peas which she forgot about). We will be leaving *Free Time* for a week in a couple of days, so we are trying to use up everything in the fridge. I dread to think what we will do with the lonely packet of frozen peas now the risotto opportunity has passed.

St Alkmund's Church, Whitchurch

Wednesday

We have come to an agreement with the weather; it can rain at night in return for reasonable sunshine during the day. So far, the weather is keeping to its part of the bargain. Once again we had heavy overnight rain but by ten o'clock it had cleared. Off we went, fortified by porridge, which Pam insists we have for breakfast at least every other day. Now I like porridge. A sprinkling of salt and a little milk is how it should be eaten. Pam, on the other hand, has a spoonful of jam with it; each to their own. There is not a lot between Grindley Brook and Barbridge apart from some really lovely countryside and the village of Wrensbury. There were not many boats about today. The journey to Wrensbury was uneventful and relaxed. We stopped for lunch, wandered into the village for a paper and listened to *The Archers* at lunch-time. The afternoon was equally quiet. The canal has frequent locks, which appear at regular intervals and add to the journey's interest. It culminated with four locks in quick succession at the end of the Llangollen Canal where it joins the Shropshire Union Canal. This little flight of locks is supervised by a lady lock-keeper. We were the last boat through before she finished her shift and had a few days off when she would visit her elderly mum. It's amazing the information you can pick up with only a brief acquaintance. We turned left at the "Shroppie" and retraced our route back up to the outskirts of Barbridge. We moored up behind a hire boat inhabited by an American couple from Jacksonville, Florida. They seem to have had a hard day and were exhausted from enduring our "cold" summer. I think they were snowbirds who had lost their way. We had a risotto (again), but this time with frozen peas (a lot of them; however, they are defrosted). We have almost empted the fridge. We made a brief visit to the pub, The Olde Barbridge, before heading back to the boat to pack for tomorrow.

Des-res on the Llangollen Canal

Thursday

We were about a mile from the boat yard where I had arranged to leave *Free Time* for next week. They would do an engine service and a minor repair to a fender eye whilst we were away. I was not best pleased to get a telephone call at ten o'clock from the yard to say they did not, after all, have a spare berth for the week. They did, however, suggest that we moored up just around the corner at British Waterways twenty-four hour moorings. They promised that they would square it with the BW lineman, look after the boat and do the servicing. We set off at once to "bag" our spot. A little nifty manoeuvring to get *Free Time's* port side onto the canal bank at the T-junction and we had the prime mooring spot. It looked fairly secure and was close to the boatyard. It now remains to be seen whether we have a parking ticket from BW when we get back next Friday. I have organised a car to pick us up at three o'clock to take us to our hotel at Manchester Airport for our early morning flight tomorrow. Monte Carlo or bust.

Busy Barbridge junction

Friday 2nd June

The more observant amongst you will have noticed that the date has skipped a week. This is due to our excesses in Nice, Monte Carlo, Cuneo and Turino. We had truly a "fab" time. A lot of our friends and their spouses turn up, as well as an old friend of ours, Brian, who lives in Cuneo, which is about a three-hour train journey from Nice. We spent a few days in Nice, went to the Monaco Grand Prix, and then crossed the border into Italy for a few days, staying in an elegant hotel in Cuneo. The Piemonte province is breathtakingly beautiful, with its rolling countryside covered in vineyards in the foothills of the Alps. My mid-year resolution is to explore more the wines of Piemonte (the two best known in the UK are Barbera and Barolo). The flights back went according to plan. Our little man picked us up at the airport and drove us back to *Free Time*, which looked remarkably well despite being abandoned for a week. I searched very diligently for a parking ticket. There was none and her engine had been serviced and cleaned. Not pushing our luck, I walked around to the boat yard to pay the bill (don't ask…) and cast off before we could be nabbed by a passing British Waterways' warden. We cruised at a gentle pace about five miles down the canal to Nantwich. There were no visitor moorings vacant, so we moored in an empty space amongst the permanent moorings (we obviously have got the knack on illegal parking). We walked the half mile or so into town to buy some provisions to re-stock our denuded fridge. Nantwich is a typical Cheshire market town: pleasant if unremarkable. We had a light salad and no alcohol this evening. The saying "I will diet tomorrow", which we have been using for a week, has now come to fruition.

Free Time III ????

Pam and Brian in Piemonte

Saturday

We awoke to a gloriously sunny day. We fiddled around a little before setting off due south at ten o'clock. We drifted along at little more than tick-over speed due to the large number of moored boats in this area. After an hour we reached the two locks of Hack Green. We moored up, and went off to explore the Hack Green Secret Nuclear Bunker. This was a Royal Air Force WWII communication centre. At the start of the Cold War, our government, in its wisdom, decided that if there should be a nuclear holocaust (not an unlikely scenario at the height of the hostilities with the Russians), then the great and the good should have a "nuke"-proof bolthole. These elite people were not defined to the proletariat, nor was the very existence of these strategic bunkers revealed to the masses, hence the advertising blurb of "secret". One can only assume that questions might be asked by the local bricklayer and his chums if they knew that in the event of a nuclear strike they would fry whilst the local MP, mayor and perhaps any royalty in the area would be secreted away below ground with all the life support systems needed to prolong the rightful governance of this green and pleasant land (well, perhaps it wouldn't be quite so green after a thermo-nuclear bomb).

Anyway, it was totally fascinating. The horrors of any nuclear war are unthinkably horrendous. The question of Iran, and its current leadership, is very pertinent here. Having got that off my chest, we had yet another salad (no booze) and set off again. We moored up at the village of Audlem for the night. Audlem consists of a number of pleasant houses grouped around their 15th century church (Pam reckons I am getting too much of a fixation on taking photos of churches, so I have not chosen it for the journal. However, I can send one to anyone upon request...). This stretch of the canal has fifteen locks in succession. We completed three locks, and then stopped at the pub below. We can complete the other twelve locks tomorrow.

Shroppie Fly - a popular pub

Sunday

We decided to set off relatively early to complete the twelve remaining locks before it got too busy. We were foiled after only one lock, when a boat with an elderly couple (I know elderly can be a relative term) pulled out in front of us and proceeded to hold us up for the next ten locks. However, they were exceedingly pleasant and kept apologising for their speed, or lack of it. Even I could not be a grumpy old man in light of such amicable people. Just before the last lock, there was a parking place which they pulled into for a well-earned coffee break. They looked a bit like our Snow Birds whom we met last week: knackered! We carried on, completing the twelve locks in two and a half hours. I helmed most of the way as *The Archers* omnibus was on the radio; I needed to catch up with every day life at Ambridge. The Shropshire Union Canal is quite narrow in places, but always has interest and not a little beauty. We got a clear run at the five locks at Adderley, breezing through like the well-oiled canal team we have become. We arrived at Market Drayton at one o'clock, and had a spot of light lunch on board. I had seen a TV programme on BBC World whilst in Cuneo about WiFi. It effectively said it was rubbish. Apparently a wet dog passing between the WiFi source and your PC could affect reception. I dismissed this as typical overstated hype. I needed to do some internet banking, so having been given the name of a pub in Market Drayton, The Clive and Coffyne, by Brian, our son in Sydney (the wonders of modern communications), I lugged my laptop into town and had a pint whilst trying to connect. I could only get an intermittent signal. It turned out the signal came from a quiz machine in the corner, so I moved closer to it. All went well until the barmaid's boyfriend went to play on it. He had long, dank hair and I lost my signal. It looked to me that he was there at least until the barmaid finished her shift, so I gave up. I should have known better than to doubt the Beeb. I will try again tomorrow, or go to the library.

Market Drayton is a fine town. The canal has some interesting wharves and warehouses. The town has many splendidly restored black-and-white timber-framed buildings. Its most famous son was Clive of India, hence the name of the pub above, although I have no idea about the Coffyne connection.

An inhabitant of Market Drayton

This completes yet another week. So far our summer sojourn on *Free Time* has clocked up 200 miles, 208 locks and 63 swing bridges in the record breaking time of 193 hours. For those who are not mathematically erudite, that is very slightly over an average of 1 mph. Now that is what I call relaxed.

W/c Monday 5th June 2006

Free Time (with washing drying)

Monday

We walked back into Market Drayton in the morning to get Pam's glasses fixed (she had stood on them) and send off last week's journal via the library. After filling up with water we continued our journey south at eleven o'clock. The "Shroppie" is a relatively recent canal, being built in the mid-19th century. It is very much along straight lines of cut and fill. This may sound a bit boring, but in practice is fascinating and extremely atmospheric. If there was a hill, then the navvies cut a wedge out of it; not the pansy burrowing of tunnels, but the serious business of cutting great wedges out of rock and earth. The spoil from this huge amount of cutting was then used to build up embankments to stride across any countryside which did not meet the required altitude for the continuation of the canal levels. The deep cuttings can only be marvelled at in awe at the immense amount of material that had to be manually dug and blasted. There are bits of the cut that are so deep that they have never seen the sun for 150 years. The ferns are splendid to behold and even beat the fernery in Sydney Botanical Gardens.

We climbed the five locks at Tyrley. This is a little bit of a bottleneck with boats queuing to go up and down the flight, and a natural chatting area as you pass the time with other boaters, moaning about the weather (which was good), the state of the toilets on the canal (which was bad), the competence of boat hirers (which was mixed), the attitude of boat owners to hirers (which was also mixed), and generally righting all the ills of the world. The bit of excitement for the day was when we came across a little narrowboat which was firmly grounded at the side of the canal at a shallow spot. There was a very elderly couple on board who patently did not have the muscle power to pole themselves off the shoal area. They had been stuck fast for some time and were despairing of ever seeing civilisation again. We tied up against them (on the deep side) and pulled them off the shallows. Our halos glowed for the rest of the day. We moored up for the evening at a village called Gnosall. An evening constitutional around the village judged it to be pretty but forgettable. Perhaps our senses, or indeed memory, have become jaded in retirement.

A double bridge, the boat we rescued and an interesting location for a telegraph pole, all in one picture

Tuesday

The sun was beating down again, as we set off fortified with Pam's porridge. The day, we knew, was going to be leisurely. Although we had thirteen miles to travel, there would only be one and a half locks. The half lock is a little dinky thing with only six inches rise. It was built at the junction of the Shropshire Union Canal and the Staffs and Worcs Canal to stop one company pinching water from the other. We stopped at Brewood for lunch. The village of Brewood is indeed ancient, originally being a Roman fort. Apart from constantly winning the Village in Bloom competition, Brewood is very handsome indeed, sporting elegant and very old buildings all around the village square. Even the new buildings are built along the black-and-white timber-framed style. One of the oddities is Speedwell Castle (see photo on next page). It was built in 1740 by the local apothecary (is that a posh name for a chemist?) who, rumour has it, won a lot of money on a horse race betting on the aforementioned Speedwell. He used his ill-gotten gains to build this remarkable folly/home. It is also rumoured that the village square is riddled with underground passages leading from each of the local pubs to Speedwell Castle (even I found this last bit a little fanciful). The mooring at Brewood is truly idyllic. It is secure, set in a wooded cut and very, very pretty, although the sunshine always enhances memories. I replaced a damaged fender eye, and polished my brasses. Now, the brasses have not been polished for a fortnight, so I was really getting withdrawal symptoms. However, we knew we needed to be at Autherley Junction overnight in preparation for tackling the Wolverhampton twenty-one locks first thing tomorrow, so reluctantly we dragged ourselves off at around five o'clock. This latter trip took us an hour and half and again passed through some wonderful countryside. We even met a boat from Ripon that we knew, so we stopped for a few moments for a chat. We moored opposite a boatyard on the outskirts of Wolverhampton. We have traversed from one of the most rural, pretty canals to the urban conurbations of Wolverhampton and Birmingham, better known as the Black Country. It remains to be seen exactly why it is called the Black Country, but it doesn't sound nice...

Speedwell Castle, Brewood

Wednesday

We decided to have an early start to get the "dreaded" Wolverhampton twenty-one locks over with and find a safe mooring in the ferocious "Black Country". Now, my dictionary's definition of prejudice is "an opinion that is not based on reason or experience". I am prejudiced about most things. An innate silly gut feeling usually proves me right (well, in my eyes anyway). In this case I couldn't have been more wrong. The Wolverhampton twenty-one was a delight. Each lock and corner showed something of interest. We actually turned one corner to find a multi-story car park filled with chaps (and, no doubt, chapesses) on the top floor peering down telescopes. Great, I thought: there must be a bird rarity in the area which I too could tick. But, no; they were overlooking Wolverhampton train station and ticking their own little lifetime train list. Not for the first time I was forced to think "Each to their own..." We had turned off our countrified "Shroppie" Canal onto the urban "Birmingham Canal Navigations". There were a number of surprises. The first was that instead of the muddy canal water we had been used to for the last two months, with the singular exception of the Selby Canal (Uncle John may remember this from two years ago), we had sparkling clear water. We could see the bottom (not very far from the top), the plants and a myriad of fish life happily darting in and out of the weeds. Although we were cutting through the heart of Wolverhampton, the canal was a little linear green park which was both marvellous and refreshing, even in the shadow of the town's incinerator. The most feared objects, the local inhabitants, were entirely friendly, although I did have slight reservations about those drinking from cans of lager at seven-thirty in the morning. Another surprising thing was the number of coconuts floating in the canal. Coconuts are definitely not indigenous to the UK. They, as far as I know, cannot be forced in poly tunnels. I am told it is something to do with Asian festivals which, for some obscure reason, necessitate throwing vast quantities of coconuts into the UK equivalent of the Ganges, i.e. the BCN, as it is known locally. We moored up in the early afternoon at a delightful spot in the grounds of the Black Country Museum. This is a huge outdoor museum recreating life at the turn of the century as it would have been in, you guessed it, the Black Country. We sneaked in for a preview and made friends with a huge Shire horse called William. Unfortunately, we did not have any carrots, so the aforesaid William was not that impressed. We will do the full tour of the museum tomorrow and, if forced, pay an entrance fee.

Pam outside a 19th century Chemist (no, we don't know who Emile Doo is, but we will ask tomorrow).

Thursday

Someone up there is turning the temperature control up a notch or two every day. We awoke to yet another hot, sunny day. This one, however, was going to be a "scorcher". Pam immediately downgraded our duvet from a 9.5 tog to a 4.5 tog. I do not understand these technical terms but am quite happy to accept Pam's judgement on such matters. We planned to spend the day at the Black Country Museum, so wandered around very happily for several hours admiring the reconstructions of life at the turn of the century. We walked into Tipton mid-afternoon for replenishment of provisions, the notable one being tonic water, of which we had none. Tipton is a suburb midway between Wolverhampton and Birmingham. Now here's the thing. There was no discernable difference between the Black Country Museum, which is a world class reproduction of life in the early 1900s, and the suburb of Tipton in the 21st century. I photographed the building on the next page, which turned out to be a pub. It reminds me of some of the remnants of pubs in the seedier area of Sydney from the same era (but, I have to confess, the type of pub I like). I swear to the temperature controller, that we were passed by a black carriage hearse, duly pulled by two magnificent black horses in all their finery, and led by two humans, also in black and also all in their finery. Pam would not allow me to take a photograph as she reckoned it was both bad luck and also showed lack of respect (besides which she could not get the camera out of her voluminous Colombian handbag in time). On returning to the boat, we went back into the Black Country Museum, had traditional fish and chips fried in traditional beef dripping, and drank copious amounts of beer to cool down (well, I did anyway). We are currently sitting in the sun, reading the papers and, of course, writing the journal. After *The Archers*, we will cross to the other side of the canal to water *Free Time* and treat her to a pump out.

Tipton Pub

Friday

The temperature controller up there has once again turned the heat up a few notches. We cast off just after eight o'clock and began our four-hour journey into Birmingham city centre. We travelled along the original BCN line, aka. The Old Line or Wolverhampton Level. The canal was surprisingly quiet. We only passed three boats all day and they were all in the last hour. Obviously they rise late in these parts. Now some brief facts: in its heyday, the BCN had more than 160 miles of canal. Even after the closures in the 20th century, there are currently more than 100 miles of navigable canal left. This is significantly more than Venice, or any other European city (unless you know better...). Birmingham city centre (as opposed to the suburbs) is very fine indeed. Perhaps some of the redevelopment could be more sympathetic (a good proportion of the city was destroyed during the war), but there can be no complaints about the café society they have constructed around the infamous Gas Street Basin area where the canals meet. We had dinner in Café Rouge. This is a chain of restaurants (perhaps franchised) which I particularly like. It is in a northern French/Belgian style; relaxed, with good food and reasonably priced. After dinner we went to the theatre (the cinema showing *The Da Vince Code* came a close second). The Birmingham Repertory Theatre Company was presenting John Godber's *On the Piste*. This was a comedy about the relationships of a couple of couples. I found the production (and indeed the play) to be lightweight and only mildly amusing, although the rest of the audience appeared to enjoy it immensely, especially with the background music from Abba. However, the stage, incorporating a dry ski slope, was both clever and imaginative.

Canals and Motorway crossing on The New Line of BCN

Saturday

Today was a pottering around Birmingham day. We wandered happily from coffee shop, to shop, to pub, to shop, to restaurant, to boat. It was all very relaxed and pleasant. Today was the opening match for England in the World Cup. Now, here's the thing. I am totally ambivalent about this event. On the one hand I really do not like the jingoistic flying of the St. George's Cross from every car window, bedroom window and flagstaff. However, I do accept that this feeling is totally irrational and if the same thing was happening in a Scottish city with the St Andrew's Cross, then that would be alright and a little puffing out of chests would be in order. Having lived in England for thirty years, and their being our closest neighbours, I really am trying to be rational and reasonable in wishing them every success in their adventure. The BBC and other television channels are not being as objectionable as usual (or perhaps I am maturing a bit) so I will support England in this World Cup. We watched them beat Paraguay 1-0 and enjoyed the victory (no hate mail, please). We were picked up by friends who live in Birmingham, who whisked us off to their local Chinese restaurant for the evening. This establishment, Henry Wong, served extremely good food; no glutinous stodgy fare laced with monosodium glutamate. We finished the evening in Colin and Sheryl's house, sampling some Macallans.

Birmingham Town Hall

Sunday

Colin and Sheryl joined us at ten o'clock, and we set off for a pleasant day's cruise in the sunshine. The canal meandered out of Birmingham, passing through the botanical gardens, the university campus and the Bourneville chocolate factory. The disconcerting signs by the canalside effectively say, "This is still an urban canal, so if you leave your boat remove anything valuable otherwise the thieving inhabitants of this area will run off with everything" (I paraphrase here slightly). We did not leave the boat, so still have all our valuables. Colin insisted on taking the tiller for the whole of the trip. He was a little like "Cool Hand Luke" in his vice-like grip of the tiller. I am sure his hand has formed a rigid claw like which will take several weeks to ease. The day was hot and sunny, the wine pleasant and flowing, and the canal shady, pretty and thankfully not flowing. A thoroughly excellent day was had by all. We moored up some fifteen miles outside Birmingham in Hockley Heath, an up-market little village, beside a pub serving Sunday roasts. Colin and Sheryl whistled up their chauffeur (their son, Mark) and we said our fond farewells. We looked forward to a quiet night watching TV and catching up on the journal.

Cool Hand Colin

W/c Monday 12th June 2006

Free Time

Monday

The hot humid weather brought some heavy thunderstorms early in the morning, delaying our departure from Hockley Heath to about ten o'clock. Some silly sod (the same one that left a windlass in Leeds) this time left a cup of tea (full) at the canalside at Hockley Heath only to remember a half-mile further on; still, the walk back to retrieve the cup did me good. Despite the heavy downpour of rain, the heat and humidity built up again very quickly which was bad news, as we had to descend the twenty-one Lapworth locks and lift two bridges in short order. We conveniently completed the last lock at two o'clock, just in time for *The Archers* and a spot of lunch. It was oppressively hot. I wrung myself out and had my second shower of the day before saying goodbye to the Stratford Canal and side-stepped onto the Grand Union Canal. The Stratford Canal is a narrow gauge canal and very pretty with a somewhat circuitous routing, mainly through woodlands. It may be pretty, but it is also very slow. We were now on the M1 of canals, the Grand Union, which is the main route from the Midlands to London. This is a wide, straight(ish), deep, and in your face canal. You zip along at the momentous speed of 3.5 mph, the countryside a blur at that speed. We literally tunnelled under the only village en route, Shrewley, and moored up at the top of Hatton Locks. We were a little drained physically (some would say mentally) after our exertions on the morning's lock wheeling. The Hatton Locks also number twenty-one, but these are W...I...D...E locks with bloody great heavy mitred gates and enormous paddle gear. Methinks we will have another gruelling day tomorrow. This two-mile stretch of locks is aptly overlooked by a very grand mental asylum on a hill. Not for nothing is this flight of locks known as "Stairway to Heaven" (predates Led Zeppelin).

Strange Lock-Keeper's Cottage at bottom of Lapworth Locks

Tuesday

Another boat turned up and offered to do the locks with us. This is normally good news as two boats fit in each lock, and there would be twice as many crew to effectively halve the work. That is the theory. This falls down slightly if the boat you are travelling with is single-handed, which is precisely what the curiously named *Doinmein* narrowboat was. We could not flatly refuse the poor chap and wait until a less numerically challenged boat came along so we politely accepted. We decided to tie *Doinmein* and *Free Time* together so only one helmsman would be needed, leaving two people to wheel the locks. This worked very well and we breezed through the twenty-one locks in a record time of two and a half hours. We stopped at a canalside garden centre to restock the various tubs and baskets we have on the boat, which were beginning to look a bit tatty and past their best. After depleting our daily budget on bedding plants we were soon to reach Warwick and Leamington Spa. These two elegant towns almost run into each other. The canal skirts Warwick not encroaching to within a mile from the city centre. It does, however, have a number of boat yards and good visitor moorings. The canal goes almost through the centre of Leamington Spa, but for some reason this famous spa resort turns her back on the canal. It is like a long forgotten route into town which is guarded by industrial estates and the back of warehouse walls. Undaunted, we chose to stop overnight at Leamington Spa. We walked into town in the afternoon and admired the Royal Pump House, the fine Regency façades and walked in some of the many parks. We finally got to see *The Da Vinci Code* in the evening. Despite the panning it received from the critics, I enjoyed it immensely. It is a long film at almost three hours, but the time did not drag at all (and no, I did not fall asleep). The basic premise of a blood-line from Jesus Christ and Mary Magdalene surviving even today is obviously tosh, but the film still manages to be entertaining, clever, thought-provoking and controversial.

This is the tattiest boat we have yet encountered

<u>Wednesday</u>

The weather had finally broken as we awoke to a grey overcast day. Although not as hot as the last couple of weeks, it was still warm enough for my knees to remain out for the world to see. After our exertions of the previous day, we decided to have a lazy day. After a leisurely breakfast (bacon as a treat) we set off and quickly left the outskirts of Leamington Spa. The Grand Union Canal is very rural here, running mainly through wooded areas. We even passed under the Fosse Way. For those of you who don't know what that is, and I was one before I read the notice, it was/is the ancient Roman road linking Exeter and Lincoln. We ascended the Bascote Locks (only ten locks today) before mooring up outside a pub aptly named The Two Boats in the village of Long Itchington for lunch. Long Itchington (now isn't that a strange name which has you scratching?) is what I consider an archetypical English village. It is a very up-market village built around a large green with the obligatory duck pond. It has no less than five very twee pubs all serving food, and one shop, which I think says it all about disposal incomes in these parts. We are off to joins the toffs this evening in one of the pubs for dinner. I am practising my accent and laugh already.

Not untypical dwelling in Long Itchington

Thursday

The sunny weather had returned. We knew we had a long day, so we set off at half past eight, went up one lock and stopped at a boatyard to be refuelled. The fuelling point was a little out of the way and did not dispense litres, only gallons (I am not sure that is legal, but hey ho). We are eating locks now.

We started at breakfast and did the Stockton ten broad locks (done on our own), had the Calcutt three broad locks for elevenses (this time shared with another boat manned (womanned?) by a very pleasant quiet little man and a very unpleasant vociferous large lady), and Napton nine narrow locks for lunch (being narrow, you have to do these on your own). The Napton nine is the start of the narrow Oxford Canal. This is one of the oldest canals. It hugs the contours of the landscape, twisting, turning and generally making you very dizzy. It is also a beautiful canal which meanders through one of the most remote areas we have yet encountered. Despite being in the relatively southern county of Oxfordshire, the canal does not touch any human habitation. It wanders around for some ten miles or more and does not pass a house, a road, a railway or anything apart from field upon field, most of which appear to be "set aside". Apart from the occasional boat, it is as if you have the whole of the county as your own personal fiefdom – a remarkable feeling. We moored up in the middle of nowhere to watch England play Trinidad and Tobago in the World Cup. We would have gone to a pub to watch it, but there wasn't one. Now here's a thing; despite being in the most remote countryside yet, we had the best television picture yet, receiving in crystal-clear Technicolor all five channels (yes, Channel Five as well, which no one can receive anywhere in the country). Why is that? In the middle of the industrial north, you are lucky to see through the snowstorm on most of the channels. There are lots of people in the north, but relatively crap TV reception. Here we are in the south in the most remote parts of the county, but you get TV reception which is faultless. Should this little fact be added to the north/south debate? I think it requires more investigation, don't you? After watching England labour to a 2-0 win, we set off again at seven o'clock to try and find some civilisation to moor up at for the evening. Two hours later we arrive at Fenny Compton Wharf: lots of boats, a pub, but still no houses.

Footbridge to nowhere on Oxford Canal

Friday

Hot and sunny, again; boring, isn't it? We continued heading roughly south as the canal continued to wend its way generally in the required direction. The canal is not so heavily locked, so a more relaxed time was had by all. We stopped at a stunningly attractive village called Cropedy for bread and water (bread for us, water for the boat – I thought I would clarify that, as it sounds as though our budget was forcing us into starvation diet mode). We also bought a watermelon. Cropedy was the site of a significant battle during the Civil War where the Royalists recorded one of their few victories. We stopped for lunch on the boat at a predictably remote spot (there was no choice). We arrived at Banbury by mid-afternoon and moored in the centre of town. I had a preconceived idea that Banbury would be a mini-Leamington Spa; it is nothing of the sort. It has a strange eccentric mixture of buildings and architectural styles which belies the fact that Banbury is a very ancient town made famous by the nursery rhyme and spiced Banbury cakes. I feel I should be more impressed than I was. This nagging feeling of disjointed thinking in the borough was confirmed when we tried to book tickets for the theatre to be told there was no production on a Friday night. Could we come back on Saturday?

Banbury Cross of nursery rhyme fame

Saturday

Despite being right in the centre of town, the night was very peaceful with no late-night revellers to hear of. We did hear the French market being assembled quite early in the morning, but that was all right. I stepped off the boat and bought some very smelly sausages (good for two months, I am told) and some

Greek olives (yes, I know, it was a French market). We had a leisurely breakfast. Pam went off to find a present for her latest niece, and I had a wander around Tooley's historic boat yard and Banbury museum. We set off into the wilds of Oxfordshire mid-morning. The day was yet again hot and humid. We were running a little short of beer, which was a major disaster. I was relegated to drinking white wine spritzers. The Oxford Canal does not go through many human habitations; perhaps there are only a few villages in the whole of Oxfordshire, never mind canalside. Having had a surfeit of the splendour of the canal scenery, I decided today was going to be a natural history day. I was going to get into the zillions of dragonflies and damselflies hovering above the water. Having consulted my Reader's Digest Complete Spotter's Guide to British Wildlife and Flowers, I now know that there only about ten or so species of Odonata order of insects in the UK, as they are collectively known. This should be a piece of cake for a renowned twitcher such as me. However, the little blighters will not stay still long enough to count the body bands, examine the wing pattern (all four of them), or even see the colour of their eyes, and the females are cunningly a different colour from the males. I have two definite ticks, the Emperor Dragonfly and the Banded Demoiselle, and about a dozen possible ticks which makes more than the British list. I think I will stick to ticking birds (saw two green woodpeckers today). Interestingly we saw two red-clawed crayfish (dead and floating but ten miles apart). These are not indigenous to the UK but apparently arrived in the bilges of ships from the Americas. They were first recorded in the River Thames and are rapidly spreading north through the watercourses, to the detriment of our puny native species of crayfish which it can easily beat up. I think there may be a culinary opportunity here. On a similar nature theme, whilst we were going under one of the few roads we encountered on the day (admittedly it was the M40) we came across a herd of forty or fifty cows, all standing alongside the canal in the tunnel under the motorway. This was very odd. I initially thought the farmer had penned them up ready for milking, or perhaps the market. Further investigation showed that they were not penned at all, but had a huge, very green field to wander about in, eat the grass, chew the cud and do whatever cows do. The only conclusion I could envisage on why they should be herded together in a noisy underpass under a major motorway was to escape the blazing sun. I guess the milk yield will be down today. The above recounting of the day's activities is a little long with my pontificating so I will draw it to an end. We moored up at a village called Upper Heyford in a spectacularly beautiful canal setting, and needless to say wandered up to the only pub to re-hydrate ourselves with a few beers. A good day all round.

Cows having a paddle

Sunday

We were joined by our friends, Lyn and Neil, who live in Milton Keynes. They drove over with their bikes on the roof of their car which we put on the roof of *Free Time* (the bikes, not the car). We had not seen Lyn and Neil for some time, so a lot of chatting went on until we caught up on what has been happening with each of us. Lyn is a doctor (not medical) and Neil is professor at Cambridge University. Now, is that impressive or not? The day was slightly overcast, but still very warm. We set off at noon, and stopped an hour later for water (boat again), lunch and at a boatyard to buy a China hat for the chimney which we had knocked off on a very low bridge. We had a delightful afternoon chatting, with Lyn explaining to me the different types of dragonflies and damselflies; she is a biologist after all. Sadly, they had to leave about six o'clock and we waved them off as they rode off back down the towpath on their bikes. It took us six hours to get to this point. They reckoned they would be back at their car within an hour. We carried on for an hour to yet another pretty mooring in a village called Thrupp. Our son, Garry, had told me that there was a WiFi hotspot in the local pub, The Jolly Boatman. If you receive this journal on Sunday evening, then he will be right. Both Brian and Garry had phoned me during the day to wish me a Happy Father's Day, which was nice. It would have been even nicer if pressies had been forthcoming, but they assure me that they had no postal address.

Pam and Lyn

W/c Monday 19th June 2006

The other *Free Time*

Monday

It was an effort to get up this morning. By the time we woke up, showered, had breakfast and watered up *Free Time*, it was pushing eleven o'clock. Still, there was no rush today as we had only planned to go the six miles into Oxford. The canal is now straighter, and very much less scenic. After about two miles we came across another *Free Time* (pic above). It was moored under a bridge and looked as though the owner had set up a bit of a workshop on the towpath. I subsequently found out that the owner was one of the "scruffies" (more later), who was more than a little eccentric. He apparently moors up in the Oxford area at various spots and then proceeds to spend a week or two cleaning up the canal and towpath in the area. His only vice is that apparently every now and again he "kicks off", whatever that means. As we approached Oxford, the number of residential boats increased. These boats are very hippy looking indeed, as are their inhabitants. Dreadlocks, Jesus sandals, ankle bracelets and taffeta skirts are the order of the day, for both men and women. We stopped at a boatyard for a pump out to be given the local gossip on our friend on *Free Time* above, and the "problem" of "scruffies", aka. hippies. The locals regard them as troublemakers, weirdoes, spongers and a general blight on the towering spires of Oxford. I, having had no real experience of them, find them to be endearing, interesting and definitely adding colour to both the canal and the town. We walked around Oxford in the afternoon, poking our noses into the various colleges and generally savouring the academic atmosphere. It is a wonderful town; the only drawback being that with its huge student population the average age looks like it is fifteen (I am sure it is older, but like policemen, students look younger to me each year). We went to the cinema to see *Poseidon*, a remake of the original classic disaster movie of some thirty years ago. Despite being based on the book by Paul Gallico, who is an excellent author (my aunt Audrey gave me a book by him called *Scruffy* when I was 13 years old), it does not have much of a story but the special effects are indeed spectacular. I swear water was lapping at my feet all through the film. The cinema was followed by pasta and a bottle of Barbera D'asti (I told you I would be getting into Piemonte wines). A good day all round.

Exeter College quadrangle

Tuesday

For the first time, we had a bit of canal rage this morning. A cantankerous git in a boat behind complained, loudly, about our recharging the batteries at quarter to nine in the morning. I thought that was a perfectly reasonable time to start the engine and also thought he was being unduly difficult. I expect he thought the same of me. Once again we walked around Oxford, soaking up the atmosphere as we wandered through the various colleges. In the afternoon we went to Oxford University Natural History Museum. The attraction was threefold. Firstly, the building; although only 150 years old (notice the use of "only") it is an award-winning neo-gothic design. The inside is supported by marble pillars and covered by a glass roof, giving the exhibits natural sunlight. Secondly, it purports to house the remains of the famous Oxford dodo, namely the head and a claw. In fact, they were casts of the aforesaid head and claw. The originals, I suspect, were hidden away safely somewhere in the vaults. Thirdly, it was free. A weather front was forecast to come through mid evening, so we elected to stay in and watch the World Cup on the TV. England once again laboured, but came away with a draw against Sweden. I thought they were flattered by the score, but the draw was good enough for them to win the group.

Oxford's own Bridge of Sighs

Wednesday

Today was the day of a major "twitch". Having passed through Thrupp a couple of days ago, much to my chagrin Pam read in her Daily Mail that a Scops Owl had taken up residence in the village, and we missed it. We had passed through blissfully unaware of the excitement. Now for those who do not know, a Scops Owl is a major rarity in the UK. It is a small owl which should be in the south of France and Spain at this time of year. This particular specimen must have taken a right turn rather than a left turn at some stage in its migration. Having done Oxford, we retraced our footsteps, or should it be wake, and returned the six miles north up to Thrupp. We moored up early afternoon and walked into the village to see what the fuss was about. There was a solitary twitcher who had driven up from Devon and had been there since half past five in the morning. He had not seen a thing. However, the thing about owls is that they tend to be awake and fly at night, and quietly snooze in a hole somewhere during the day. Once this dawned on us, I did not feel so bad. We fiddled around cleaning the boat for the rest of the afternoon before venturing out to owl spot after *The Archers*. The Scops Owl has a peculiar song. It is a single monotone (can a monotone be anything other than single?) which sounds a bit like a sonar bleep. Apparently, it had been bleeping for weeks, forlornly seeking a female to bleep back at it. As it is only encountered in the UK once in a blue moon (well, at least ten or more years) it had a fat chance of a hot date in Thrupp. The locals thought it was a security alarm somewhere which kept going off until its call was recognised by a visiting birdwatcher. It was actually seen for the first time a few days ago. It is incredibly difficult to spot, but once on the move it is infuriatingly easy to hear. Our solitary twitcher had swelled to a baying mob of more than a hundred maniacal would-be tickers (yours truly included). After a lot of chasing from tree to tree with spotlights, the mob finally got a reasonable sighting about eleven o'clock at night. This is my 359th UK tick, and the first for almost two years. The goal is 400 ticks, when I can join the elite 400 club. At the current rate of ticking, I should achieve this in the year 2086 when I will be 135 years old.

Where is that damned bird...?

Thursday

We awoke to sunny, but very windy weather. After a walk to the nearest shop some half a mile away, we set off around ten o'clock to go back into Oxford and re-acquaint ourselves with the various scruffies (hippies) we had passed twice already on our travels. This time we locked up onto the River Thames instead of going into Oxford city centre. This point, called the Duke's Cut, is the furthest north the River Thames ventures. We followed it upstream more or less south-west as it twists and turns through open countryside. A combination of the exposed topography, the strong wind and the fact we were headed into the south-westerly wind most of the time made for a slightly uncomfortable passage. As the afternoon progressed, the wind began to abate.

The river is very pretty as well as being remote. It reminded me a bit of a warmer version of the River Ouse between York and Boroughbridge. One of the advantages of the Thames is that the locks have keepers to do all the heavy work; I should hope so too, after the hefty fee I paid to get a fifteen-day licence. We moored for the evening at Bablock Hythe. There is nothing here apart from The Ferryman Inn. It was mentioned by Matthew Arnold in *The Scholar Gypsy* in 1853, and actually has a passenger ferry across the Thames. Now here is a little known fact. This ferry has been running since AD904. It looks a bit tatty, but somehow I don't think it is the original.

Boats are bigger on the Thames

Friday

Hot and sunny, again; boring isn't it (I actually wrote that for last Friday's journal, so no change there then)? The wind had gone, and what a difference that made. This part of the English countryside is really very attractive. It does not compare with the rugged splendour of the Scottish West Coast or the Highlands and Islands, or indeed with the Lakes in Cumbria, but nevertheless it is still attractive. It seems to be more genteel and generates a safe feeling. I cannot imagine a howling gale with associated rain or snow and ice to chill your eyeballs here in the soft south. An overnight stay in this area holds no fears. No, this is the gentle south, and I like it. We continued our cruise upstream, winding around in ever decreasing circles, savouring the views and wondering what would be around the next corner, of which there were many. The dragonflies were once again out in numbers after the winds of the last few days. The birds were twittering, the fish a-leaping and generally we were at peace with the world (until a pesky cold caller tried to sell us an upgraded Orange phone). We travelled a full twenty miles today and went up seven locks, which I think is a daily record. However, it was a joy, and no effort at all, despite going uphill, so to speak. At the last lock before our destination, Lechlade, we were advised by the lock-keeper to remove our various flower pots from the boat's roof as the cows tended to try and eat them in the middle of the night. How considerate of him to tell us, we thought, until he added that the cows couldn't quite reach the flowers and then overstretched themselves and fell into the river. The lock-keepers are then called on to try to fish them out. Now here is another little strange quirk about this recommended mooring. You moor up at a field which is in Oxfordshire, you walk along the towpath for about 200 yards which takes you into Wiltshire, you then cross over the river by road bridge into the tillage of Lechlade (remember tillages?) which is in Gloucestershire: three counties in two minutes. Lechlade is a large village/small market town. It cascades down to the river with associated antique shops, chandlers, numerous pubs, a few shops, but not a single hole-in-the-wall cash machine. However, the main grocery shop does do "cash back", which is a concept I knew little about, and certainly had never used before. Having tried it, and liked it, I will return tomorrow morning for some more.

Lechlade church steeple

Saturday

There was no rush in the morning, so we walked into Lechlade at a leisurely pace: a few provisions, morning coffee and yet another purchase of a hat for the chimney at the chandlers (we've lost two this trip). We set off at midday and continued for about a mile to the limit of navigation on the River Thames. Having turned around in quite a tight space, all we have to do now is go downhill all the way to London on the Thames, some 146 miles away. The day was yet again hot and sunny as we retraced our way downstream. The trip was delightful and enlivened by a little plastic boat which was hired for the afternoon by four personable, but slightly inebriated Irish gentlemen. They were completely out of control, careering around at great speed: very entertaining. There were concrete pillboxes every half-mile or so along the river. I could not find any reference to these in any guide book, and can only assume they were some form of defence erected during WWII. Why, I have no idea, as strategically the Thames does not appear to go anywhere, but I had visions of Captain Mainwaring and his jolly troop of *Dad's Army* volunteers manning their concrete defence posts with both vigour and enthusiasm. We moored up at a place called Newbridge which consists of, surprisingly enough, a bridge and a pub at either side. The pub we visited, enigmatically called The Rose Revived, had extensive grounds rolling down onto the river. It being a hot, sunny Saturday afternoon, the staff was stretched and stressed with a high volume of punters quaffing huge quantities of beer and ordering mountains of food, all with chips on the side. We watched the World Cup on their outdoor screen: very continental.

Limit of navigation on the Thames

Sunday

We actually overslept this morning, not waking up until after nine o'clock. However, we had planned a fairly relaxed day, so I guess we started as we meant to continue. After breakfast we set off around ten o'clock, just in time for *The Archers* omnibus. The journey down-river was just as enchanting as cruising up. The corners were still acute, the countryside wonderful and, no, no one had moved the pillboxes. Today was another wildlife day, and in particular we were concentrating on imports from foreign parts. In last week's journal I referred to red-clawed crayfish. We were now encountering scores of crayfish traps, all with their orange floats bobbing around in the water. Having weaved our way through them without once fouling the propeller, I asked the next lock-keeper what they are about. They are put there by the Environment Agency to try to stem the crayfishes relentless march (or should it be crawl) from the stronghold of the Thames through to the rest of the waterways throughout England. The evidence of our two previous sightings suggests this strategy has failed. The lock-keeper told me they were American. We also came across a family fishing for crayfish for the cooking pot; and, yes, they too told me they were American. Their fishing technique was to put a bit of best bacon in a Tesco poly bag and lower the bag to the bottom of the river, leave for ten minutes, and then haul the bag back up to the surface, complete with half-eaten bacon, and red-clawed crayfish which is about to be eaten. I told you there was a culinary opportunity here. Yesterday we saw a Little Owl (this is a distinct species as opposed to an owl which happens to be little). It was sitting on a fence post almost within touching distance as we cruised by it. The Little Owl was introduced to the UK from mainland Europe in the mid 1800s by wealthy landowners who thought they were cute, would enliven their dreary lives, and not be a hazard by occupying the ecological niche of a native species (although I don't think they gave the last bit a lot of thought). In any event, they were right on all three points and the Little Owl is now established in some numbers (and they are exceedingly cute). The third foreign import is the dreaded North American mink. We have not seen any, but there is no doubt that the swelling population descendent from escapees from mink farms are a serious threat to native wildlife and the water vole in particular. There are lots of floating wooden platforms with rectangular boxes in these parts. Again, after enquiries with the lock-keepers, I have discerned that Oxford University are doing a mink census by baiting the boxes and placing Plasticine on the bottom of the boxes. A quick regular inspection will tell them how many mink have been a-visiting. I suspect that it is only a matter of time before these census boxes are converted to traps and an eradication programme is undertaken. We moored up in early afternoon at Godstow, site of the now ruined 12th century nunnery. Off to the pub to watch the World Cup.

The crayfish family

W/c Monday 26th June 2006

Free Time

<u>Monday</u>

For the first time since darkest Wales, we awoke to a grey drizzly day. It was not wet enough to put on waterproofs, but Pam did have her hood up for most of the day. Admittedly she had just washed and dried her hair, so I guess a potential frizziness factor came into play. We have ten days left on our River Thames licence, so to obtain maximum benefit we will take the full ten days to reach the tidal limit of Teddington, London. This is an average of just over ten miles a day, so there is no great rush to go anywhere for the next week or two. We departed Godstow about nine o'clock and cruised through Oxford yet again, but this time on the river rather than the canal. There were a number of excellent moorings on the river which we will remember should we be in this area again on *Free Time*. The river splits into two channels at Folly Bridge in Oxford. We took the narrower channel and weaved our way through and by a number of buildings which were built as follies on the midstream island. It was all wonderful stuff and deserved more in the way of an exploration. Just south of Folly Bridge are the rowing club buildings of the various colleges of Oxford. I kid you not, there must have been twenty to thirty very large boat houses, all in a row. Methinks that there has been an awful lot of money "invested" in Oxford University over the years. It was along this stretch of the river that we saw a young man on a bike with floats on it, furiously peddling away and going at a great rate of knots. Pam was too embarrassed to take his photograph without first asking permission, so you will just have to take my word for it. We moored up for the day at lunch-time at Abingdon. We walked into town, in the rain, and did a little shopping. Abingdon is an attractive 18th century market town, although the abbey dates back to AD675. There are a number of really great buildings and rambling old staging inns, but once again the town is spoiled by the ubiquitous modern pedestrian precincts and its associated tat architecture.

Civic buildings, Abingdon

Tuesday

The weather resumed its usual course of hot and sunny as we set off around ten o'clock. First stop was at a boatyard to replace a gas cylinder and then on out of Abingdon heading roughly south. Once again wildlife was prominent during the day with a number of kingfishers, no less than five red kites and, the surprise of them all, a little Muntjac deer. Although yet another foreign import, it was very endearing being only two feet tall. It was a particularly good spot, as these deer are secretive and usually only venture out in deep woodland. We were also witness to a major punch up between a squirrel (grey) and a crow (black). Each gave as good as it got, so after four rounds, I guess it was a draw. However, the best came last. As we were within a few miles of our destination, Wallingford, we spotted a huge, gigantic, dinner plate sized (well, about eighteen inches diameter which is large) terrapin basking on a log at the side of the river. Having consulted my local wildlife expert, i.e. the lock-keeper, I now know that these are yet more imports being released into the wild some years ago by disillusioned pet owners. They are not exactly thriving, but some individuals are doing OK and growing to extremely large sizes. Their numbers peaked about two years ago and my sighting was the first this year (gold star to me then). They are not believed to be breeding, so are not a long-term threat to any indigenous species. Still, I was very chuffed to see it nevertheless. We moored up at Wallingford and walked into town. Wallingford is a very fine ancient town which received its royal charter in 1155. Sensible planning conditions have preserved the town centre and its magnificent multi-arched bridge across the Thames. We were expecting Pam's nephew, Colin, and his wife, Jacqueline, and daughter, Wing, that evening, so we went re-stocking in the local branch of Waitrose. The mobile phone went as we were gaily pushing our trolley. It was Jacqueline to say they had arrived in Wallingford. They were in the car park of a supermarket called Waitrose, and were they close to the boat?

Readers may remember the mystery of why the Thames was fortified by pillboxes every half-mile. Chatting to a neighbour on our mooring, I now know why and am happy to share this with all interested parties. What I had stupidly failed to notice was that all the pillboxes are on the north side of the river. They are not in fact guarding the river route as I thought, but form a line of defence across the Thames. Should the invasion have taken place, and the Home Guard on the cliffs of Dover failed to stem the initial wave of German invaders, then Plan B would have been to fall back to the other side of the Thames and make a stand there. Now you know.

Houses are getting very grand on the Thames

Wednesday

It is amazing how much paraphernalia and attention a two-year-old (Wing) has and needs. After some of us (well, me), had breakfast on the park bench because the boat was too cluttered, and one or two false starts before remembering that we had forgotten something, we finally set off after ten o'clock. The Thames was absolutely delightful: wide, handsome and not a little magnificent. The houses continued to be awe inspiring, the villages chocolate-box pictures, and the wildlife showing off as though there was no tomorrow. More foreign imports were flaunting themselves, vying for attention alongside the indigenous species. Red kites and kingfishers are old hat now, but along came the young imported upstarts in the Egyptian geese, Canadian geese and Mandarin ducks. Jacqueline was enthralled by all the birds and held tight onto my binoculars all day. I feel sure that with a little sage coaching I could turn her into a class act in twitching. Wing was a delight. She had taken to "Aunt Pam" big style and insisted on being with her all the time. This included toilet visits. To me Pam had drawn the short straw here, but she smiled through it all. We stopped for lunch at Goring (a nice little English village) and continued to Pangbourne, arriving early afternoon. We moored up in the picturesque water-meadows and walked into town to buy provisions for the barbeque. Colin acted as master chef for the barbeque. That's the thing about barbeques. It is a bloke thing to light the fire, turn the steaks and sausages, and generally poke around in the smoke. It is a woman's thing to marinate the meat, do the salads (and washing up???) and, for once, generally play a subservient role. Wing flitted from role to role. It is nice to have them around.

Jacqueline and Wing looking happy

Colin looking happier

Thursday

As forecast, each day this week has been hotter than the previous one. Pam and I did a little early morning shopping in Pangbourne, allowing the Henderson family a little space to wake up and sort themselves out for the day. The plan was to only cruise for three or four hours to Sonning, just past Reading. However, as the Hendersons are leaving on Saturday, I thought we would push on to Henley for the night, which meant that Jacqueline could see Windsor Castle on Friday evening. Now, without getting too lavatorial, when Pam and I are on our own we usually go two to three weeks before the dreaded pump out. However, now Colin, Jacqueline and Wing are here, the holding tank gauge is shooting into the red sector with alacrity. So there was a pump out and water in Reading and then a slight detour by going down the Kennet and Avon Canal for a mile or so to let Jacqueline see what a canal looks like, and to give Colin a chance to operate a lock on his own without one of those nice Thames lock-keepers doing all the work. The planned overnight stop at Sonning became our lunch stop, only there was no mooring space left. We continued for an hour or so, looking for somewhere to park. Having failed miserably to do this, and our tummies were definitely revolting at this enforced delay, we stopped in the middle of nowhere and headed for a likely tree branch trailing at the side of the river. I despatched Colin with a rope and a knife between his teeth (I lied about the latter) to make the leap and wrap the rope around the branch. This he did and we had a very pleasant lunch gently bobbing at the side of the Thames with only the sharp end tied to a tree branch. We arrived at Henley late afternoon, only to find out that it was Regatta Week. Now that was quite exciting and very, very swish (although Colin, obviously an inverse snob, was complaining about the cut-glass accents, the posh outfits, the straw boaters and the stripy ties). I let him take the helm and work off some of this prejudice by threatening to ram any boat which dared to come within ramming range, and there were loads of those. The only problem here is that a narrowboat is very slow; even the punts were outrunning us, never mind the very sleek Thames craft which are prevalent at these events. Another side issue was, of course, that there was no room at the inn. We had to head on well past Henley to Medmenham before we came across the first available mooring spot. This is a very attractive hamlet with a number of houses all well above the million pound mark. It is the site of the 16th century St Mary's Abbey (still more or less intact), and also where the infamous Hellfire Club met. There are no shops here, but we did go to a very old (14th century) up-market pub for dinner called The Dog and Badger, (what an evocative name) which looked after us very well. We didn't see any likely Hellfire Club members, but dinner was good.

Yet another one that got away

Friday

Hot and sunny, again; boring isn't it (I actually wrote that two weeks ago, and again in last week's journal, so <u>still</u> no change there then)? Our intention was to reach Windsor that evening; it was some seventeen miles away, so yours truly got up and set off on his tod just after eight o'clock, leaving the rest of the team soundly asleep. After a decent interval, orange juice, tea and a bacon and egg roll arrived for the lonely helmsman. It was another delightful day's cruise through stockbroker belts and old-moneyed areas. The houses were very grand, particularly around Marlow: nothing under £1m here. Colin helmed some of the way, although he did have an altercation with a river-trip boat about who had the right of way around a sharp corner. I hadn't realised he knew so many Anglo-Saxon words. I had seen yet another foreign import, several ring-necked parakeets, the previous day, and was determined to let

Jacqueline tick these off today. Although I saw one first thing (before the crew had got up) there was not another sighting all day. Jacqueline had a go at helming, and after a bit of confusion about left and right, she generally settled in to doing a good job. We arrived at Windsor mid-afternoon and moored up on an island under the ramparts of Windsor Castle (with a pedestrian bridge) about a ten minute walk out of town. Windsor is all it is reputed to be: very touristy, quaint, an eye for the main chance, and I like it. Jacqueline has decided she would like to stay another day, and having been given permission by the skipper, informed her husband of the fact – typical woman.

Jacqueline bird-watching and helming

Saturday

This was my kind of day. We didn't go anywhere, and the Henderson family and Pam decided they were going to "do" Windsor Castle. I decided I was definitely not going to "do" Windsor Castle so retreated out of the sun into a hotel with a high ceiling in the restaurant with ceiling fans, a WiFi connection and table service: bliss. Several drinks and e-mails later everyone joined me for lunch having done half of Windsor Castle. Colin had decided he had done enough and went off, via public transport, to collect his car, which he had left at Wallingford. Pam, Jacqueline and Wing returned to complete Windsor Castle. I retired to the boat to charge the batteries (no cantankerous git in the vicinity), laze in the sweltering sunshine, have a chat to the three ladies in a motor cruiser called *Free Time* (it should have been called *Three Time* as it is the third one we have seen, counting our very own) and then watched the football, when England were well beaten by Portugal. Windsor on a Saturday was not quite as attractive as Windsor on a Friday; this is a function of the inverse proportion of the number of people visiting on any one day. The Windsor and Eton train station has been converted into an elegant shopping arcade with a goodly number of bars, shops and restaurants. There is also an old locomotive from the royal train from about 1880 on show. There is still a train station in Windsor, but it occupies the fag end of the swish arcade with only a single track line in (and, by definition, out). It makes you wonder how the Queen goes up to Balmoral today. Presumably she gets into the Bentley or Rolls in the palace, crosses the street and the royal train will be parked up on the single track, causing the odd delay or two for the daily punters trying to get in and out of London. Anyway, the swish arcade hosted a Café Rouge, so I took everyone out for a dinner of mussels and chips.

Changing of the Guard at Windsor Castle

Sunday

Colin had collected his car yesterday, so there was a great deal of activity as the Hendersons packed and subsequently Colin and I packed the car. All was in order and we waved them goodbye at around half past ten. Pam and I walked into Windsor for provisions, had coffee and set off about lunch-time in the blistering sun. It was over 30°C. We had only eight miles to travel today, but the locks were very busy as every boat in a five-hundred mile radius had taken to the water in an effort to alleviate the sweltering heat. We travelled through Windsor Great Park with its dire warnings of death by decapitation if we should even think of besmirching this royal park by attempting to moor up on it, and eventually stopping for lunch at Runnymede Park. Here we were allowed to moor; this must be a result of the Magna Carta which has not yet filtered through to the Windsor family. We had a double dose of excitement at the last lock of the day, Bell Weir Lock, just above Staines. First we had to wait as a very, very smart and elegant large motor cruiser locked up in front of us. The motor cruiser was a nice metal one; none of your plastic rubbish here. It was in fact David Suchet's of Hercule Poirot fame. I was so starstruck I forgot to take a photograph. As we locked down with another narrowboat and numerous other plastic cruisers, the other narrowboat got hung up on the lock side with a great crashing of crockery and not a little panic as the stern side went under water. Shows you how easily it is done if you are not paying attention, and the two lady attendants were definitely not, preferring to discuss what they were going to do for dinner. We moored up in Staines. This is a modern commuter town for London. Nevertheless, it is reasonably pleasant with a nice waterfront and, of course, the ubiquitous pedestrian precinct.

Staines Town Hall (now a pub)

W/c Monday 3rd July 2006

The third *Free Time*

Monday

The heat wave continued with temperatures soaring above 30° C again. We made the brief walk into Staines; the first port of call was the pub to re-hydrate, and it wasn't even eleven o'clock. I toddled off to the library to send last week's journal, whilst Pam toddled off to do a bit of window shopping. There was no great rush to be anywhere today, so we happily fiddled around until about one o'clock when we set off. We had quite a lot of washing and tidying to do after the Henderson invasion, so the little washing machine, which can only be put on when the engine is running, was on a tight schedule; but it was a very good drying day, with any wet clothes drying in the heat before we had a chance to hang it on a line (slight exaggeration here, but you take my point). The tight schedule for the washing machine immediately had to be revised as we promptly ran out of water on the first wash. The next water point was two locks away, so there were no great issues apart from only doing two out of the three scheduled washes. We only travelled eight miles with three locks before mooring up for the day at Shepperton at four o'clock. This has been for years the mainstay of the British film industry with its famous studios. We walked into the village, past the car park with four large studio vehicles dispensing wardrobe costumes, but didn't see anyone famous. We visited the nearest pub, The Three Horseshoes, for yet more re-hydration. This pub was very strange and could have come out of a film set somewhere (I subsequently found out that in former lives it has been both a police station and a morgue). It was quite small and had the usual array of artisans out in front swilling beer in the sun. However, inside there was a cast of very strange people sitting around the bar. There was the elderly deaf drunk (no, not me) who looked like he was either wearing a rug, or had his hair groomed and dyed every morning. There was a guy who looked like he was one of the Wurzles, with straw hat and lamb chop whiskers which could have been glued on. He was talking to a gentleman who looked like he had eye-liner on, or perhaps he was Surrey's only coal miner. Then there was a somewhat elderly lady in summer frock, long flowing white hair, heavy eye makeup, complete with eye-liner which extended beyond her eye and semi-circumnavigated her head and immaculate nails complete with polish, but sinisterly with one finger missing (not so immaculate there then). Could this have been some gangland act of revenge during a misspent youth? Her husband (I assume it was her husband) was also somewhat elderly but dressed in chinos, flash leather trainers and a trendy hooped T-shirt which would have happily adorned a French onion seller. There was a full supporting cast as well. I was convinced that these characters had just finished a hard shift of acting for some television drama, but no, they were just local punters in for a late afternoon drink. I can only guess what they are writing about us. Our mooring was opposite Desborough Island and, although still on the Thames, is on an obscure branch off the main navigation. The mooring is idyllic with the occasional canoeist paddling by. It is greatly enhanced by flocks of ring-necked parakeets which nest and roost on the island. There are dazzling flashes of electric green, but they are somewhat noisy. This is OK for visitors, but I guess they drive the locals nuts as they never shut up whilst flying.

One of many houseboats in this area

Tuesday

The temperature was even hotter than yesterday. Once again, we had a late start at ten o'clock and a very relaxed eight mile journey with two locks down to Hampton Court Palace. We were very grand and moored up at the jetty for the Palace. The place was buzzing with the Hampton Court Palace Flower Show. We had a quick change of clothes to our Sunday best and a light lunch on board and then went off to the Flower Show. There were all sorts of large launches arriving with loads of people, so we felt very privileged to walk the thirty yards or so from *Free Time* to the entrance of the Flower Show. This feeling was quickly deflated when we found out that today was the first day of the show and only open to journalists, TV presenters, invited members of the Royal Horticultural Society and, of course, any passing royalty who happened to be in the area. As we did not fall into any of these categories, we had to blag our way through (give or take £40). This is a very major flower show, second only to Chelsea. The emphasis is less on show gardens and more on retail stands, and is more of a "hands on" experience, It was not too busy and, not being a general public day, there were lots of freebies. My favourite was the Plymouth gin stand, but Crofts Sherry and the wine stands were not far behind, although we did have to pay £8 a pint for a Pimms (No1 with mint, cucumber, orange and lemon for you aficionados out there). The plants, stands and displays were very impressive; so impressive that the only thing we bought was a bottle of twelve-year-old balsamic vinegar and a single estate, Sicilian bottle of olive oil. This was after a careful tasting session, with Pam having the final word.

Pam at the Hampton Court Palace Flower Show

Wednesday

This was a longish day, especially after being pampered by the Thames lock-keepers. We awoke a little ahead of schedule to thunder and a rainstorm. This passed quickly, but the forecast was for more heavy showers. It was still very hot and humid, so rain was welcome for once. After mopping up, we set of at eight o'clock aiming to arrive at half past nine at Teddington Lock, which is the start of the tidal stretch of the Thames. We arrived a little early to catch the tide, but locked through anyway and punched the tide for half an hour or so before being whisked off towards Brentford. A sharp left hand down a bit, and we were back on the Grand Union Canal. We skirted around the suburbs of London and battled up a dozen fairly heavy locks; mind you, all locks that you have to do yourself are heavy after the luxury of the cheery Thames lock-keeper doing all the work. We shared the locks with a rather posh couple in another narrowboat called *Sonoma* (something to do with Californian wine apparently, but I had never heard of it). This couple had a wonderful dog, a bearded collie, which seemed to wander around with half a field in its coat and ears. I couldn't work this out until about the third or fourth lock, when I saw it rolling and wriggling around on its back in the long grass. It also took a shine to Pam (a bit like Wing). Harry (that's the bearded collie) would quite happily get on board *Free Time* and stand beside Pam as she helmed the boat into the locks. His owners said that was the first time he had ever got onto a strange boat. I wondered exactly how strange they thought *Free Time* was. We did a do-it-yourself pump out (not as nasty as it sounds), filled up with water and parked up about half past five at a marina in Cowley Peachey, which is in Uxbridge, a suburb of London. We intend to stay here for about a week and just commute into central London and chill for a period before Garry joins us in about ten days' time. We have electricity, a pub and restaurant a few metres away, utility block and water point. We do like the finer things in life. We went off to the Water Edge restaurant as we have run out of food on board. The meal was excellent. We watched the Portugal vs France World Cup semi-final. I was supporting Portugal until their players started throwing themselves around in demented frenzies trying to con the referee into giving them unfair free kicks and penalties. I switched allegiance after two or three of these blatant cheating efforts. I never thought I would be supporting France because I thought they were the more honourable team. Our waitress was wearing a Portugal flag around her waist. I guess she was not a happy bunny after the result, not helped by my meagre tip. I am a would-be pensioner, you know.

Hampton Court Palace (and Pammie)

Thursday

What an exhausting day. It started in leisurely fashion. We lay in bed and listened to John Prescott getting an ill-mannered grilling from John Humphrys on the *Today* programme. We had a light breakfast of orange juice, crackers and honey because there was nothing else left on the boat. After showering we walked to West Drayton railway station, which was about a twenty-minute walk away. We took a train into Paddington Station, which is only a fifteen-minute train ride. Then it got exhausting. Do you notice how tiring it is wandering around city streets? You can walk all day, every day along the towpaths, across the country parks, wandering around villages without a thought, or a twinge, or a whinge. Walk a tenth of the distance in a city and you are knackered. Is it the chewing gum on the pavement acting as an energy sapper? Is it all the pollution from the traffic making your lungs work overtime and producing the soporific effect? Or is it the fact that you have to weave, duck and dive, accelerate and slow down, dodging all those people and all that traffic? And that is another thing. Where do all these people come from, and what do they all do for a living? How can any nation, country or region support all this mass of humanity? City slickers may be wealth creators. I am sure they are, and jolly good at it too to be able to afford the inflated London prices, but just how they do it is not obviously visible to me. However, I digress, again. We wandered around Paddington, Little Venice and down Edgeware Road looking in the zillions of Middle East restaurants in this section of Arab land in London, although we settled for a traditional English pub which served surprisingly good home-made food. After Hyde Park we were both exhausted and decided to head back to the boat. I fell asleep on the train back, but Pam prodded me at the right station. We got some provisions at the supermarket before lugging our poly bags back to the boat for well earned G and Ts. Methinks it will be an early night tonight.

Surprising what you come across, even if it is the Irish spelling

Friday

The hot and humid weather had finally broken. It was a lot fresher and a little drizzly. After our exertions of yesterday, we decided to do a little day cruise. The marina is on the junction of the Grand Union Canal and the Slough Arm which branches off in a westerly direction to, surprisingly enough, Slough. Now all the canal guide books are a little dismissive of this five-mile stretch of canal. Some of the descriptions include words such as "uninteresting", "boring", "almost straight line", "dull housing", and "industrial estates". We knew that the terminus of the canal was not in the middle of town. These same canal guides described Slough as being "a new town, undistinguished architecturally and with no discernable town centre". This must be the reason why the canal doesn't terminate in the town centre then, but on the plus side, there were no locks. So, undaunted, we decided to "do Slough". These somewhat derogatory comments obviously had put off all would-be boat travellers along the Slough Arm. There were none, nor, judging from the vegetation growth, had there been for some months, nay, years. Now here's the paradox; as there were no boats moving, partially due to the uninteresting, dead straight canal going nowhere, the canal was no longer uninteresting or dead straight, but I suspect still went nowhere. The margins of the canal had blurred and softened as the vegetation had taken over without the passage of boats to keep the channel clear. The other issue was the name "Slough". Who dreamt that name up? It sounds like a reptilian skin-shed, or perhaps a very slow-moving, lazy mammal. It does not conjure up any attractive visions of the mind with such a name, a bit like its counterpart in the north, "Bingley". First impressions were that the canal was a delight. With the heavy vegetation, you could not see any dull housing or industrial estates. In fact, it is quite countrified, sweeping easily over several aqueducts and through long cuttings. The total width may indeed have been almost straight, but the narrow channel dictated by the incursions of trees, reeds and general green stuff was certainly not straight tasking the helmsman's skill. Like life, the joy was in the travel and not the final destination. After all, who wants to arrive at the destination for an appointment with the grim reaper? Better to travel without actually getting there. However, the speed gradually reduced as the weed got thicker and thicker. The water was crystal clear, so we could see the increasingly dense obstacles, as well as the bottom getting closer to the top with each mile. Now, as we never have that much speed to begin with, any diminution is bad news. We were down to about two knots when we arrived at Iver, which has a very large colony of residential boats sitting two or three abreast in the canal. These boats had not moved for a number of years. My immediate thought was that with these boats the channel must be clearer there. Not a bit of it. The weed was almost impenetrable in the narrow channel between the boats and the bank. As we were almost stationary, we decided to turn at the next winding hole, although we were still a mile short of Slough Basin. We arrived back at the marina in time for lunch and *The Archers*, but we never did see the non-existent town centre of Slough. Over my G and T in the evening, reflecting on why the channel was absolutely clogged at the residential boats where intuitively you would have thought it would be at its deepest, I concluded that the houseboats were merrily discharging their grey water into the canal. This would be the shower, washing machine and washing-up water. The phosphates in the detergents used would act as fertiliser for the weeds, promoting growth and effectively cutting Slough off from the delights of boaters and, of course, vice versa. I wonder who got the better deal.

The Slough Arm

Saturday

We visited Kew Gardens today. We took a train and effortlessly, give or take two changes, arrived at Kew Gardens Underground station. The area of Kew has a leafy village feel to it. The streets are clean and green, there are nice chintzy coffee shops, fantastic organic food shops and very desirable, but modest (relatively) housing. The actual Kew Gardens became the Royal Botanical Gardens in the 18th century, and jolly nice they are. The scale of these gardens is huge, with 300 acres of gardens, plants, follies, palaces, ponds, cottages and, of course, pavilions. If you have never visited, I urge you, do so. It is well worth it and certainly relaxing, and depending on how fanatical you want to be, absolutely fascinating. The breadth and number of plants housed here is breathtaking. Now I am no botanist and have difficulty in telling the difference between an oak tree and a fir tree. All the species are well labelled and have little quirky facts written alongside to keep the plebs, like me, interested. For instance, did you know that the banana tree is not a tree at all? It is in fact an herb with aspirations above its status. The palm-like tree is just tightly wrapped herb leaves. Now you know. Kew Gardens also sports an Orangery, almost identical to the one in Vienna, complete with the excellent restaurant. The pavilions have to be seen to be believed and are a tribute to the Victorian vision and pretentious delusions of grandeur. They are magnificent homes to the tropical collections. The modern Princess of Wales Conservatory, which I am sure is very clever in design and ideal in creating the correct conditions for its exhibits, just does not have the extravagant scale or indeed the gravitas of the Victorian-designed buildings (unnamed Victorians because I don't know who they were).

The Palm House, Kew Gardens

Sunday

Since we left Ripon at the beginning of April, today was the first proper Sunday. We rose late, had bacon sandwiches for breakfast, listened to *The Archers* omnibus, read the Sunday papers from cover to cover, and went to the Water Edge restaurant for dinner and to watch the World Cup final. Bliss, busy doing nothing. Having done nothing, I have nothing to write about. I could discuss (which means giving you my opinion) the guilt or otherwise of NatWest Three, the completely one-sided extradition act with the USA cravenly conceded by David Blunkett, Tony Blair's belated and ineffectual intervention and, worst of all, Baroness Scotland's attempt on radio to present this huge, huge government blunder as being fair and equitable. I could eulogise on the merits of the ageing French team and the scandal-ridden Azzurri. But fear not, I will sign off another week without comment.

Packet Boat Marina

W/c Monday 10th July 2006

Free Time

Monday

Once again we did nothing today, so nothing to report, so I won't report it, bar telling you that we walked into West Drayton, found it closed, so walked back again. I walked into Yiewsley and had a haircut in the afternoon. We do lead such exciting lives.

Yes, another church. St Matthews, Yiewsley

Tuesday

Normal service was resumed today, and we departed from our comfy marina heading into central London. The London wildlife is quite interesting. Three things strike me. There are lots of grey herons. But these are herons with attitude. They are not like the country scaredy-custard herons that fly off if you so much as come within half a mile of them. No, these are the butch version. They stand at the canalside and stare you down as you approach. These macho herons do not fly off; they stand their ground and see you off their patch. I think the message is clear, "Don't mess with me!" We also saw our first urban fox. It was out and about at ten o'clock in the morning, which I think is past its bedtime. It was bold as brass and had a bit of a scratch as it watched *Free Time* cruise by. However, it did look a bit mangy compared with the pristine red foxes you get in the country. Perhaps this individual was atypical. The third strange thing about London wildlife is the fishermen. Now normally, but admittedly not always, fishermen on canals are taciturn and will avoid eye contact at all costs. As we slow down to pass them, they will find anything to do rather than lift their heads, acknowledge the boat and, God forbid, say "good morning". At any potential contact with human beings, or perhaps just boaters, they will find an urgent need to re-bait their hook, or perhaps be totally absorbed in unscrewing their thermos flask or, if this has failed them, just stare morosely at their navels. However, the aforementioned rules do not apply to London fishermen. They are gregarious and chatty, smile, and never fail to wave and shout out a greeting. Their accents tend to be thicker than most, so I am assuming that it is indeed a greeting, or some such jollification. Although we were travelling into the heart of London, as usual a canal route gives the impression of a ribbon of green spearing its way through the urban sprawl. We travelled fifteen miles today, but had no locks. This took us five hours, give or take a stop at Sainsbury's. We passed the rebuilt Wembley Stadium, heading towards BT Tower. Although we had been travelling through suburbs for hours, the arrival at Little Venice took us by surprise. Suddenly there were rows of boats at either side of the canal. The area has a colourful and almost Bohemian atmosphere. We found a space without too much effort and moored for the night. I spotted another boat from Ripon a couple of boats along. We knocked on their door and had a chat for a bit. We strolled into Paddington and found a pub called Fountains Abbey with WiFi. We left it too late to go to the theatre or cinema, but there is always tomorrow.

Little Venice, London

Wednesday

It was another gloriously sunny day to explore Little Venice. This is a particularly pleasant area with wide leafy streets, well-kept elegant houses, hanging baskets for the world and, of course, the canal setting. It has a number of very individualistic shops, tearooms and Victorian-style pubs and dining rooms. Don't you like that term, dining rooms? It is like being back at school, only with a butler in attendance. We strolled, had coffee, and strolled some more before descending on a secluded, very elegant garden centre. Pam has very fixed ideas on potting out yet another flower container which she has painted *Free Time* blue. White pelargonium it is then. We took the Underground into Charing Cross. We had time for a quick visit to the National Gallery to see van Gogh's *The Sunflowers*. My brother, Iain, and his wife, Margaret, along with Ann and John may remember, or perhaps not with the amount of alcohol that was put away on that trip, that we saw this painting at its permanent residence at the Vincent van Gogh museum in Amsterdam about fifteen years ago. It is currently on loan to London, and I am pleased to report it is just as yellow. We bought tickets for Mel Brooks' *The Producers*, aka. *Springtime for Hitler,* and checked out where the theatre was before ambling back through Covent Garden to get the Underground back to the boat for some serious container planting and paper reading (you can work out who did what), accompanied by the odd glass of wine. The theatre ticket price included dinner, so off we went quite early for our meal and thoroughly enjoyed our evening. *The Producers* is a musical comedy which, apart from being a spectacular production in the large, exquisite Theatre Royal, Drury Lane, is funny, entertaining and absolutely irreverent – in fact, typical Mel Brooks.

Trafalgar Square (and Pammie)

Thursday

We enjoyed Little Venice so much that we decided to stay an additional day. We walked around the various shops and street markets in search of a large glass jug suitable for Pimms. Now, there are a lot of jugs out there, but you would be surprised at how many Pam can turn her nose up at; she can be infuriatingly fussy at times. Never fear, good old Woolworths eventually came to our (well, my) rescue. We looked in at the local cinema to see what was on this evening. Whilst I quite fancied *Pirates of the Caribbean*, I was not prepared to pay the outrageous London prices for a cinema seat. We will save this up and watch it en route "up north" at half the cost: a small price to pay for a principle here. After a leisurely lunch on board and reading of the newspaper, we set off for Paddington Station. Pam went shopping for food in Sainsbury's and M&S (both situated in the station) whilst I picked up my e-mails. Garry and his friend, Kath, are joining us tomorrow night and it would never do not to have sufficient food for at least 5,000. Pam obviously had not heard of the five loaves and two fishes story, so we have everything, including the kitchen sink. The fridge door only shuts with a lot of effort. Our metal teapot started leaking this morning. I spent at least an hour trying to plug the leak with a soldering iron. Whenever I chased down one leak, another appeared in the seam of the spout. Eventually I gave up, so I guess we need to put a new teapot on our shopping list for tomorrow. It was pleasantly warm today, if overcast. The forecast for the foreseeable future is hot and getting hotter.

Houseboat in Little Venice

Friday

As promised, the weather was hot and sunny, but a little too breezy for my liking. We were foiled a little in our planned early start, as there was a queue at the water point. Come ten o'clock we were off in earnest; we cruised out of Little Venice, detoured into Paddington, went straight through the middle of Regent's Park Zoo, through Camden Town, around the back of Euston and King's Cross, and then reached the Islington Tunnel. As a tunnel, this is not particularly remarkable at only slightly more than half a mile in length. What made it remarkable was that our tunnel spotlight would not work. There was a slight panic before we got out the handheld spotlight which we plugged into the cigarette lighter. Pam did a sterling job of standing at the bow in the pitch dark and pointing the searchlight up at the tunnel ceiling and side. I subsequently discovered that in addition to the on/off switch beside the helmsman there is also a sneaky little on/off switch on the fixed spotlight itself which had, entirely of its own volition, moved to the "off" position. I didn't tell Pam this, just that I had fixed the light! The journey up to and including Islington was a delight with interest at every turn. However, as we journeyed further into the hinterland of London's East End, the scenery became more menacing with security bars, razor wire and strange tattooed men with stranger tattooed pit bull terriers, or akin to something of that ilk. However, we had no problems and arrived at Limehouse Basin by mid-afternoon. This is in the heart of the old dockland and the new yuppiedom. The basin itself is quite pleasant, as is the surrounding area. There are a small number of nice restaurants, cafés and pubs within walking distance. There is still a huge amount of building work as developers continue to sell one-bedroom flats for more than £300k. It is a little incongruous to have high security, trendy developments cheek by jowl with the council housing estates of Stepney, Tower Hamlets and Bow Common. However, it does seem to work and everyone just seems to rub along quite happily. The time was now ten o'clock in the evening. My usual routine was to complete the daily journal, drain my malt whisky glass and be tucked up in bed by half past ten. However, Garry and Kath say they will be arriving shortly before midnight. Pass me the matchsticks and I will try to keep my eyes open until then.

Me looking nautical

Saturday

Today was going to be both the pinnacle and literally the turning point of our trip. This was the fabled trip up the Thames. It is the ultimate trip for any narrowboater. It is held in awe by all us flat-bottomed-boat owners and will be the subject of dinner stories for years to come (be prepared...). We rose about nine o'clock ("we" being Pam and I). It took a good hour and a half rattling around before we could get Garry and Kath to stir. We had a great fry-up breakfast and then a twenty-minute stroll to Canary Wharf. Now all you doubters out there who just know they hate Canary Wharf and all it entails, you are wrong. Like me, you probably have never been there and hate the mere concept of it. Once visited, you will love it. As Kath said, it is like a mini-Manhattan. The skyscrapers tower above as they are meant to do, the streets are wide and leafy, there are little green squares at regular intervals, transport links are great and, of course, there are all the underground malls. Don't knock it until you have tried it. It is indeed a city within a city and has a very different feel to it from the general London experience. We locked out of Limehouse with the tide at a quarter to four. The tideway was both very busy with trip boats and private boats and had a distinct chop to it caused by a combination of a brisk easterly wind and all those trip boats churning up the water. The trip was exhilarating. Apart from the chop, the tide swished us up to and under Tower Bridge. We rubbed shoulders with battleships, catamarans, Edwardian cruisers, and police launches. The trip, all three hours of it, fully deserved its reputation. Each mile held its own delights, including being shooed out of the seventy-five-metre exclusion zone for the Houses of Parliament. After Westminster Bridge the number of trip boats diminished and the river flattened out leaving a smooth passage. Pam was thankful of this having taken the brunt of a wave breaking over the bow, resulting in a full, and I mean full, change of sodden clothes to a drier variety. We came off the tidal way at Brentford and locked through two locks to berth up for the evening. A short walk down Brentford High Street found us a busy Italian restaurant. It was good to see Garry and Kath again, and they seemed to have enjoyed their day.

Garry and Kath approaching Tower Bridge

Sunday

Once again the skipper was up and about before the crew stirred. I reversed *Free Time* back 100 meters for another DIY pump out, filled her water tank had a shower and still could not get anyone to stir. Undaunted, I set off from Brentford and finally shamed everyone into getting up. Pam, Garry and Kath eventually got up (in that order) and set about their various ablutions. We were very much on an urban canal after the wide and proud River Thames. Today's trip had a very different feel to it. Pam and I had already travelled on this section of the Grand Union Canal last week as we completed the meagre eight miles to the Boat Packet Marina. However, there were ten locks today and both Kath and Garry had not yet experienced the joys of working through a lock with only your own muscle power. We shared the locks with a single-handed skipper who looked the double of Uncle Albert out of *Only Fools and Horses*. He was both a grizzled old tar, and a very nice man to boot. He certainly knew what he was doing, and as we had four people on board, his numerically-challenged status did not present any problem. We quickly developed both a routine and a rapport. Pam and he helmed our respective boats, manoeuvring them in and out of the ten locks whilst swapping tales and sundry chit-chat, Garry and Kath worked the boats through the locks, and I walked ahead and prepared the next lock for easy passage. At the top of the summit, Uncle Albert stopped to clear his propeller of the weed he had picked up. As we bade each other farewell, he slipped me £5 to give to the "children" for their help. He would not take no for an answer; as Kath said, "How sweet!" before pocketing the aforesaid fiver. The day was very hot, so we sipped Pimms and generally soaked up the sun for the leisurely lock-free stretch to Packet Boat Marina, arriving at two o'clock. After an excellent lunch with my famous grilled tuna steaks, we cooled off with a beer at the Waterside pub before walking Kath to the station to catch a train back to London. Apparently she has to work on Monday. The rest of the Porteous family will dine out tonight.

Houses of Parliament from outside the exclusion zone

W/c Monday 17th July 2006

Entertaining on *Free Time*

Monday

We had a very leisurely morning indeed at Packet Boat Marina. Garry was still sound asleep at half past nine, but we decided to get up anyway. I strolled down to Cowley Peachey to visit the library to send last week's journal and with a small shopping list for provisions. Pam and Garry spent time together on the boat re-bonding. After lunch, Garry went off to catch a bus (yes, a public transport bus) to Heathrow for his flight home to Edinburgh. We set off in baking heat for the short journey to Uxbridge. Now for years, I thought there was no such place as Uxbridge. I thought it was an amalgam of Oxford and Cambridge, denoting a fictitious twilight satellite town of London with academic aspirations. There is indeed an Uxbridge, although it has no discernable character and is entirely interchangeable with all those other satellite towns of London. It's not that you dislike it; it is only that there is nothing to like. We toyed with the idea of going to the cinema to see *Pirates of the Caribbean*, or indeed *Superman Returns*. However, we felt it was just too hot, so we walked back to the boat and had a cold drink in the pub we are moored alongside called the General Eliot. Now, if like me you had no idea who General Eliot was, I can now enlighten you. He was the commander in charge of the defence of Gibraltar in the mid-18th century. I can only assume he was a local lad.

Yes, another church. St Margaret's, Uxbridge

Tuesday

The forecast was for the very hot weather to continue all week with temperatures reaching the high 30ºC. We have formed a cunning plan. We will leave fairly early (early being nine o'clock) and try to avoid mad dogs and Englishmen by mooring up before the temperature peaks. Accordingly we set off at the appointed time and continued our cruise back to Ripon by saying farewell to Uxbridge and heading in a northerly direction along the Grand Union Canal. Uxbridge probably marks the limit of the outer suburbs of London. The canal certainly seems prettier, more countrified, with crystal-clear water. Pam spotted an enormous fish which, judging by its ample girth, I can only assume was a mirror carp of an exceedingly mature age. We had a very pleasant cruise, passing through a number of well-spaced locks before reaching our destination for the day, Rickmansworth. We stopped at the Tesco moorings for provisions, before continuing for a very short distance to our overnight mooring. Rickmansworth is an old medieval town, although very little evidence of its antiquity remains today. The church (19th century) and surrounding buildings (17th century) are pleasant enough, but my quota of church photos has been filled for the week, so you will just have to imagine them. The town is also pleasant with all the normal amenities. Rickmansworth does not boast a cinema, but it does have a theatre, aptly named Meetwaters Theatre. We wandered round to see what was on in the evening. The bad news was that there is no production scheduled until October – very strange. The good news was that there was a tea dance in progress and we were very welcome to join in, a request we politely refused. The heat was becoming difficult, so we needed a little siesta and lots of liquid methinks.

Paddle steamer, canal-style

Wednesday

The temperature reached the all-time highest in July since records have been kept, and we were bang in the middle of the hottest place in England. It is very, very warm at 36.3° C. I was drinking copious amounts of liquid (no, not beer) and still felt thirsty all the time. According to our cunning plan, we left Rickmansworth at nine o'clock. The Grand Union Canal is wide and purposeful. The first couple of miles are lined with residential boats of every description. There are big ones, small ones, posh ones, tatty ones, brand new, wrecks, hippies, yuppies – a strange mixing pot indeed. We skirted Watford without even knowing it and continued through country parks, golf courses and the occasional estate. Cassiobury Park in particular is both grand and pleasant. It was once part of the gardens of the Earl of Essex in the 17th century, with most of the trees being over 300 years old. We stopped for lunch at the small village of Hunton

Bridge. It was pleasant enough, with an attractive church (a photo opportunity despite being over church quota) but not big enough to merit an overnight stay, so we pushed on to Kings Langley, a few miles and locks further up canal. The canal, although having lots and lots of moored boats, had very few boats actually moving. I guess this may be a function of still being in the London commuting belt. Since leaving Packet Boat Marina, we had been in the locks on our own, which meant double the work for yours truly. On leaving Hunton Bridge we managed to slip alongside the only other boat moving in our direction that day. It was inhabited by a very talkative dad with two youngish daughters, an even younger son, and a dog whose age I could not discern. There was no mum in sight. Perhaps the hubby's constant chat decided her to become the ex-wife. Anyway, the kids, and dog, were great, doing all the work (well, the dog didn't do much, but looked very willing) and with Pam doing her usual sterling job of helming through the locks, I felt redundant. We cruised serenely up the canal with so little effort that I almost decided to carry on when we reached Kings Langley. But no, a plan is a plan, so we moored up, waved a fond farewell to our lock companions and took out the ear plugs. These children, unlike Garry and Kath who received a gift of £5 from Uncle Albert, departed no wealthier than when we met them. We are on a budget you know. Kings Langley is a bit of a tillage (half way between a village and a town). It definitely has royal connections, with a couple of bodies buried somewhere to prove it; Edmund de Langley, brother of the Black Prince is one.

Hunton Bridge Church

Thursday

We only had a little hop of two miles and some five locks today as we continued our ascent into the Chiltern Hills. Our overnight destination was Hemel Hempstead. We arrived before lunch, so we moored up and went sightseeing. The first sight we were presented with was having to negotiate our way across the Plough Roundabout, known locally as the Magic Roundabout. Six major roads feed into this very large roundabout, and at each entrance, and by definition each exit, there is a mini-roundabout. Now here's the catch – you can go around the roundabout in any direction you want. None of this "after you, Claude" and keep going in a clockwise direction. No, if you feel like it, or indeed the traffic looks lighter, just go anti-clockwise. It is a horrific free-for-all, but seems to work and keeps the heavy flow of traffic moving. Apparently, when it opened some thirty years ago, policemen were placed at each of the six mini-roundabouts directing the traffic. Can you imagine modern budgetary pressures allowing this to happen today? No, just let chaos reign. Hemel Hempstead is a well planned new town (apart from the roundabout), but with a charming old town with its own High Street. The modern shops and arcades are surrounded by lots of parks and spacious playing fields. I liked it a lot. It sports a theatre in its old town hall, but once again it was between productions on the day we tried to visit. Undaunted, we walked to an out of town leisure complex and finally got to see *Pirates of the Caribbean*. It is a lavish Walt Disney production starring Johnny Depp, whom I think is a terrific actor. The screenplay is laughable, and the whole very lengthy film just a piece of hokum. However, it is done with wit, great special effects and I found the 150 minutes to be a delight.

Hemel Hempstead's Magic Roundabout

Friday

Once again it was very hot. We set off from Hemel Hempstead about nine o'clock. The plan was to double the previous day's mileage, and go four miles. This also involved the small matter of eleven locks and one swing bridge as we continued our climb into the Chiltern Hills. There was hardly any boat traffic around, so we ploughed on regardless of finding a lock partner. We came across a couple of British Waterways guys doing some maintenance on a lock. In chatting, as you do, we found out that the water quality is very poor in the extreme heat. Not only are the reservoirs very low, but the little water there was, was totally devoid of oxygen. The BW guys told me that they were furiously pumping hydrogen peroxide into the reservoirs. Now this is bleach to you and me. If the water was still low in oxygen, it would certainly clean all your clothes whiter than white. They had been testing the water and not only was it low in oxygen (very toxic), but it has blooming algae (very toxic) and botulism (very toxic). Remind me not to fall in. They were real rays of sunshine and even suggested that we should beetle off as far north as quickly as possible to prevent being trapped in the toxic south and up sh** creek without a paddle. Whilst I am sure there is a kernel of truth in this, I remained cool and decided to stick to the plan. We arrived at Berkhamsted in the early afternoon. Berkhamsted is a very pleasant country town. The remains of Berkhamsted Castle were just beside our mooring. There are only a few partial walls left standing. Its main claim to fame is that it was here, in 1066, that William the Conqueror was given the crown of England. The main town lies a few hundred yards to the south. Graham Greene was born here and a lot of his novels make references to places and buildings in Berkhamsted. Now I have never been a fan of Graham Greene, having been force-fed his novels as home readers at school. I remember the trudge of ploughing my way through *A Burnt Out Case* and *The Quiet American.* However, conversely I thought the film adaptations of the aforesaid *The Quiet American,* and in particular *Brighton Rock,* were excellent. Berkhamsted left a positive impression, being a pleasant town with a number of small independent quirky shops. It even had a Café Rouge. We dined out, courtesy of Café Rouge/Tesco gift vouchers, which Jacqueline had sent down via Garry. Thanks, Jacqueline.

Canalside at Berkhamsted

Saturday

Have you noticed how accurate weather forecasts are nowadays? They used to be notoriously works of fiction and the butt of jokes (remember Michael Fish assuring us there would be no hurricane twelve hours before the whole of the South of England was rendered treeless and overnight Seven Oaks was renamed No Oaks?). Now you listen to the weather forecast and you can guarantee that whatever they say will happen. It has not been an overnight revolution, but kind of crept up on us. Well, last night the forecast was thunderstorms and heavy rain at dawn and more storms mid-afternoon. We were wakened at five o'clock not so much by the pitter-patter of raindrops, but the full-blown version of hammering and not a little riveting on the boat's metal roof. The storm had cleared, as forecast, by nine o'clock and was replaced by the customary hot sunshine. Half an hour later we were on the road, well, to be more precise, on the canal. The Grand Union Canal still continued its seemingly never-ending climb into the Chilterns with locks every half-mile or so. However, it had become very countrified as it left behind the last town for some time. My favourite type of cruising is when we go through wooded areas. The canal takes on a character and seclusion all of its own. Although there were more boats on the move (weekend and start of the school holidays) we had still to find a lock partner. Perhaps word has got round, and like the majority of fishermen, eye contact from fellow boaters is very much avoided, and we are definitely on our own. Still, the weather was great, Pam and I have got into a well-practised routine at each lock, so we were at peace with the world. Having taken full cognisance of the aforementioned weather forecast, we moored up at Bulbourne in the early afternoon for the day and went to the pub for a cold beer. Ten minutes later the rain started. We had a very enjoyable afternoon chilling out and generally being busy doing nothing. In my case this involved a siesta, listening to the radio play and writing the journal. Pam busied herself with a bit of a boat tidying and listening to her Spanish CDs. There is not much at Bulbourne. There are some British Waterways workshops making wooden lock-gates, a forge making ornate metal structures, and a pub. It is also the start of the descent from the summit by seven locks in very short order. But that will be for tomorrow; in the meantime we will have our regulation three-mile stroll this evening to ensure we have not missed anything.

A tight squeeze on the Grand Union

Sunday

We moored up last night amongst a bunch of young live-aboards, kitted out with regulation dreadlocks and accompanied by dogs of various descriptions: dubious parenthood and one little terrier also had dreadlocks. They were all very pleasant (people and dogs), if a little spaced out. The pub next to the moorings had a Cajun evening last night with barbeque and live music. It was all very jolly, with our boating neighbours occupying a long trestle table. However, what we hadn't realised was that they were going to extend their partying to a makeshift barbeque on the towpath almost beside our boat. It continued to half past three in the morning at which time I assume the various substances ran out, or they passed out. In any event I slept through most of it, but Pam didn't. We set off before nine o'clock and completed the rapid descent through the seven Marsworth Locks before swinging a sharp left hand down a bit to join the Aylesbury Arm of the Grand Union Canal. This is a narrow beam canal, all of seven miles terminating in the market town of Aylesbury. It is completely remote but does have sixteen locks to keep us occupied. This canal is very pretty but does have very narrow channels with reeds which threaten to strangle the life out of it, very narrow bridge holes to threaten the paintwork of *Free Time,* and very narrow locks to threaten the patience of helmsman and crew. However, we arrived at Aylesbury by mid-afternoon relatively unscathed. There is a terminus basin at Aylesbury run by the local canal society. They made us very welcome, assigning us a secure berth and showing us all their facilities (showers, toilets, water point, laundry room, library, cuddly toy exchange, etc.). They even gave us a free little Aylesbury duck (not a real one, you understand). Aylesbury is a three-minute walk from our mooring. It has a fairly modern town centre with all the usual amenities. It also has an old town around its 13th century church which is an absolute delight to wander around and soak in the ambience. In the evening we went to the cinema to see *Superman Returns*. It has spectacular special effects and an incomprehensible plot. All the current crop of blockbusters seemed rather long. This one was well over two hours. I only nodded off once.

Aylesbury Arm fighting off the reeds

W/c Monday 24h July 2006

Free Time

Monday

We had decided to remain in Aylesbury for a few days, so today was very much a "chill" day. We did a little shopping and explored Aylesbury a bit more. Now for some history. The Romans constructed Akeman Street (conveniently now the A41) which runs through the middle of modern Aylesbury. There are only traces of the Roman settlement left but Aylesbury is mentioned in the Domesday Book (1086). It has always been the major market town in Buckinghamshire and is still the County capital (now, I didn't know that bit). It gained a reputation for the Aylesbury Duck in the 19th century, the breed of white duck famed for its rich flavour. Aylesbury has a Roald Dahl museum, as he wrote most of his books whilst living in Aylesbury. The

Great Train Robbery happened a few miles from here and the robbers were sentenced by the Crown Court in Aylesbury (now closed and I assume awaiting future conversion to a theme pub, perhaps Jail House Rock Café.). I went off to the Chicago Rock Café to use their WiFi hotspot, and of course had the obligatory pint, whilst Pam spied out suitable candidates for a hair appointment. We sat on the boat in the afternoon, sipped some wine, read the papers and generally whiled away a couple of hours. As the cinema was so close (and, vitally, air-conditioned in still sweltering heat) we decided to have our second trip in two days. This time we watched *The Break-Up,* starring the real life couple, Jennifer Aniston and Vince Vaughn. Now this is a bit of a girly film about the trauma and drama of a couple breaking up. When we arrived, 98% of the audience were female. I tried to look inconspicuous, but I think my white shorts were a bit of a give away. Despite being a girly film, I quite enjoyed it and now realise what a selfish, blinkered, insensitive, boorish, and chauvinistic bunch us men are (well, if you believe this inference from the film, you will believe anything).

Houses on the enigmatically named Parson's Fee, Aylesbury

Tuesday

If there was trauma and drama from last night's *The Break-Up*, it was nothing compared with today's trauma and drama. How can anyone get so worked up about a hair appointment? Well, Pam can. Do they know what they are doing? What colour should I get the hair? Will they cut it correctly? What will the sun do to it? The questions (without answers) go on for ever. Anyway, off she went for her hair appointment at nine o'clock. I spent the time getting up, showering, wandering around the monthly farmer's market in the town square, and having coffee in The Coffee Republic (in that order). Three hours later, I eventually got the phone call and met with Pam for drinks. As usual, all her fears were groundless as she, and her hair, looked great, even if she did blow our budget with one twist of the tin foil. She is now addicted to Toni and Guy. We had drinks in The

Farmers Arms which is part of what was a 14th century staging coach inn. It was elegant, cool and welcoming. Pam reckoned if she lived in Aylesbury, this would be her local, and I agree. We bought some organic chutney, farm-made sausages (garlic, sage and mutton) and some fresh bread before walking back to *Free Time* for a ploughman's lunch and a glass of wine. At the pub on the corner we had to squeeze by this young chap dressed in only shorts and an eight-foot python which, appropriately enough, was draped around his shoulders like a well-cut boa should (not that I am insinuating that the snake was drunk) – obviously a must-have fashion adornment. Now I think there is something distinctly suspect about anyone who should own a snake, never mind take it for a walk, or should that be for a slither? We gave both the snake and its owner a wide berth. It was far too hot to do anything but shelter from the sun, listen to the radio, sip wine and beer, and have the occasional forty winks. In the late afternoon we ventured out to get some provisions and for Pam to buy a hat. She did have a *Free Time* baseball cap given to us by Ann and John, but this blew overboard quite early in the trip. She needed another hat (obviously) to protect her from the blazing sun; another record high was forecast for tomorrow, so we all know it was to protect her new hair colouring, and at the prices Toni and Guy charge, I should think so as well. I will stroll up to the Chicago Rock Café to pick up any e-mails (sadly lacking as of late) and try to re-hydrate a little.

Pam and said hairdo

Wednesday

The temperature, as forecast, was high, but more importantly the humidity was also very high. This is the most uncomfortable we have felt all trip and I suspected the little washing machine would be working overtime today on the numerous changes of clothes. We waved a fond farewell to Aylesbury at half past nine and started our climb up the narrow canal to the junction with the main line Grand Union at Marsworth. At the second lock, all of half a mile from Aylesbury, we caught up with a small narrowboat aptly named *Short Cut*. "Cut" in canal parlance is the name of a pound or stretch of canal between two locks. As the boat was very small, I thought this was a smart play on words for the name of a boat. It was crewed by a fairly elderly couple, the hubbie of which was unable to close the lock gate. He had telephoned British Waterways for assistance. Whilst it was very stiff, it was moveable with a bit of a heave, so we opened it and did a bit of an overtaking manoeuvre, as *Short Cut* now felt obliged to await the arrival of the British Waterways men to explain the situation. I thought this was fair enough and, indeed, the correct thing to do. As *Short Cut* was now following us, after passing through each of the sixteen locks today, I emptied the lock behind us to ease their passage up this fairly onerous stretch of canal. This couple were very pleasant, even if the gentleman did a Superman imitation by wearing his red underpants over his shorts. This is a slight exaggeration as his red underpants extended by at least four inches over the top of his white shorts (no shirt) – very strange. We were drinking lots of iced drinks in the humid heat. You will recall we bought some garlic sausages yesterday for our barbeque tonight. We stuck the fairly well-wrapped sausages in the fridge. The garlic seemed to percolate everything in the fridge, including the ice cubes. All day we have been drinking garlic-flavoured iced water, orange juice and the *pièce de résistance*, garlic-flavoured gin and tonics. I think the major drinks companies have missed out on a marketing opportunity here. Having arrived at Marsworth by mid-afternoon, we moored up and walked to the nearest pub to take on liquid. Unfortunately, this pub was closed for the afternoon, so we had to retrace our steps and go an equal distance in the other direction to The Red Lion for beer and spritzers. Having re-hydrated (again, and again, and again), we returned to the boat for showers and only the second barbeque of the whole trip. This will eliminate the garlic-flavoured ice cubes, but perhaps we will be able to buy more in Marks & Spencer if they take up the challenge of this innovative new suggestion.

Marsworth residence

Thursday

We continued our descent down the Chiltern Hills in largely rural settings. This time we were accompanied by a very smart little narrowboat, *Madrigal* (isn't that a strange name for a boat? Apparently the previous owners were singers. A madrigal is a 16th century song for several singers without musical instruments; now you know), which was heading for a working boat rally to be held at the weekend. This made for easier working of the locks until we dropped by the wayside to fill *Free Time* with water and have a spot of lunch. The day was again very hot and humid. A slight respite was had at Grove Lock, just south at Linslade, where the lock is adjacent to the Grove Lock pub and restaurant. As Pam was driving as usual, I worked the lock via the bar and managed to pick up a pint on the way, and more importantly, was able to drink it whilst the lock was filling and emptying. We stopped for the day at Leighton

Buzzard. Now, isn't that another strange name? It sounds more like it is an elusive bird (a buzzard discovered by Jim Leighton), or perhaps a crotchety old gentleman who hails from Leighton. Anyway, the town was fine, if uninspiring. It has a great church dating from 1288, with a very tall spire (all 191 feet) and an interesting market area with a mixture of 17th to 19th century buildings. All in all it was a quiet, uneventful day (but it still flew by at a rate of knots). We are moored quite close to a 24-hour Tesco. I am really looking forward to doing a bit a shopping at three o'clock in the morning, because I can.

Leighton Buzzard Main Street

Friday

We had not very far to go today, so we had a really lazy morning. The three o'clock in the morning shopping plan did not come off, so Pam toddled off at ten o'clock. I got a phone call half an hour later to come and help her carry the shopping bags. The day was still sunny, but less hot and humid. We set off at eleven o'clock and drifted our way northwards. The Grand Union Canal here is still wide and proud, but in this area uniquely meanders in river-like fashion as it follows a parallel course to the River Ousel. It is once again very rural, and pretty to boot. Although there are not many houses around, the buildings you can see ooze affluence. After a slight altercation with two boats coming the other way about a difference of opinion on who should have shut a paddle (grumpy old men come to mind), we moored up mid-afternoon in the outskirts of Milton Keynes in a place called Fenny Stratford. We only nibbled at the edges of Fenny Stratford, not walking into the middle of town. What we saw was OK, but I guess we have not done the town justice by lazily not venturing forth. The main irritation at the moment was a boat a couple of spaces along which had been continuously running its noisy generator since we arrived some four hours ago. The term "grumpy old man" again comes to mind.

Grand Union Canal (pretty, isn't it?)

Saturday

Ann, John and Greg, the black Labrador, arrived last night. We chatted (although Greg didn't say a lot) and then went to bed, only emerging from our respective pits about nine o'clock. By the time we had sorted ourselves out, given Greg his morning walk and had breakfast, it was half past ten when we set out. It was appreciably cooler than of late, but not unpleasant. We travelled through Milton Keynes. Now, for years Milton Keynes has been the butt of jokes about its concrete cows, its interminable roundabouts and its crass architecture, and more recently the emergence of MK Dons, the transported Wimbledon Football Club. I have to tell you that all of the aforementioned may be true, but like people, you should take things as you find them and not rely on reputation. Milton Keynes is a delight with wide open green spaces. It is relatively clean, has embraced the canalside and, in my view, is exceedingly well planned and executed. Greg decided he liked sitting up on deck with the helmsman, although he did have a tendency to lie down either on your feet, or on the flowers, or both. It took us four hours to cruise through greater Milton Keynes. Mid-afternoon, Pam managed to put her back out and then had to lie prostrate on the bed for a couple of hours. She was undoubtedly in a lot of pain, but how did she manage to do in her back? Well, she was putting a jar of coffee away. Now consider this; a jar of coffee weighs, what, four ounces? We have done 550 locks on this trip, and 99.99% of those have been done by yours truly. At each lock there are between three and four lock gates and each lock gate weights between a tonne and a tonne and a half. To travel through the lock, you have to open and shut each lock, hence the total lock gate heaving (using the lowest estimate each time) is 3,300 times, or a total of 3,300 tonnes. You know what I am saying here; I have heaved, grunted, sweated and generally manhandled 3,300 tonnes without complaint (well, not much anyway) and Pam moves a four-ounce coffee jar and has to take to her bed with painkillers. Where is the equality in that and, more importantly, who is going to make dinner? The problem was solved when John offered to take us to the local pub, The Barley Mow, in Cosgrove for steak and chips for us and veggie burgers for him (I am not sure what Greg will have).

Church at Cosgrove

Sunday

Pam woke up with her back a little better, but still painful. We resolved to put her on light duties and to feed her a diet of painkillers and alcohol. We said farewell to Cosgrove mid-morning, casting off and heading north. We were immediately embroiled in a mega fishing competition, with the canal barred to all comers with a forest of carbon fibre fishing rods across the canal. Undaunted, we ploughed through them, albeit at a relatively low speed. We dutifully said "good morning" to every fisherman. Now, this is a bit of betwixt and between as far as fishermen are concerned. They obviously breed a bit of a hybrid in this area which is a cross between the taciturn northern variety and the chatty, cheery London fishermen. Some said "good morning", some felt an urgent need to inspect at very close quarters the bait at the end of their line, and some fumed at the audacity of a boat actually using the canal rather than leaving it the sole preserve of the piscatorial lovers (or tormentors). We were overtaken at this point by another narrowboat, which admittedly was doing an imitation of a bat out of hell. This was much to the chagrin of a number of fishermen, but one individual in particular was absolutely incandescent with rage as we proceeded to churn up his allotted patch of water into a muddy stew. Now, I had a degree of sympathy for him as he ranted, raged and swore at the boat which had overtaken us. My sympathy waned a little when the aforesaid boat disappeared at a rate of knots over the horizon and he began to vent his spleen on *Free Time*, which was continuing at the serene rate of 2mph. John, who was helming at the time, had no brook with such language, but had a nice repertoire of hand signals involving one or two digits.

Before we had set off, I was sent to the shops to get three items of provisions. Now, I forgot one of them. Two out of three is pretty good in my book, but Pam was not pleased. Accordingly, we stopped late morning (which was not really long after we set off) at Yardley Gobion (no, we have no idea how to pronounce it either) to shop. All of us, Pam, Ann, John, Greg and I, walked into the village to buy the forgotten bread. It was quite pleasant with thatched cottages, an elegant church, (no picture), and a cluster of housing around two or three village greens. We continued our voyage north up a series of seven locks into Stoke Bruerne. This is the archetypal canal village with houses on the canalside, pubs and gardens at each lock, a waterways museum, and about a zillion onlookers. Despite the pressure of so many critical eyes, we cruised faultlessly through the throng with everyone, Greg included, playing their part. After the crowds we were soon into the Blisworth tunnel. This is the second longest canal tunnel on the system at 3,057 yards. I was a bit concerned about how Greg would take to being in a very, very dark, noisy, spooky tunnel for almost an hour, but he was a star. He just lay down on his dog basket and snoozed.

Now Ann was a different story... We tied up for the evening at the village of Blisworth and retired to the pub, purely medicinal for Ann's tunnel nerves and Pam's bad back, you understand.

John and Greg a little lost in Yardley Gobion?

An elegant stone bridge at Cosgrove

W/c Monday 31st July 2006

Free Time

Monday

Ann, John and Greg left us today, so it was the well-drilled routine of John taking public transport (that's a bus, by the way) from Blisworth back to Fenny Stratford to retrieve his car. Off he went, clutching his bus money in his hand, whilst the rest of us just hung around, drank coffee and read the papers. John arrived back after a couple of hours. Now consider this. Since the Hendersons joined us on Friday night, we had been travelling for two days (admittedly not very long days, but long enough). John effectively retraced the journey, not with a helicopter, or even a high-powered car, but on a bus. He then picks up his own car and drives back yet again. He does this in a couple of hours, but we have been travelling on the boat for two days. No wonder commercial canal transport will never be viable again. We bade our fond farewells. Everyone looked sad, especially Greg who, I think, liked us. This may have been something to do with all the titbits he managed to scrounge off Pam at meal times.

I had booked *Free Time* to have her bottom repainted at a boatyard in Braunston next Monday. My calculations have gone a little awry, as Braunston is less than twenty miles away and we have seven days to do it in. So having established there is no time pressure there then, we took a bus into nearby Northampton for the afternoon. The bus station is in the very centre of town. We disembarked from our little bus and were immediately funnelled through a shopping centre (a clever bit of marketing/planning there) and from there onto the generous market square, which is flanked by a large number of buildings built at various times throughout the centuries. They are an eclectic lot, these buildings, with wildly varying façades of different styles. The town centre of Northampton is compact, but also relatively large, if that is not a contradiction in terms. We had lunch in a pasta house in the older part of the town opposite the Guildhall, a 19th century status building, but nevertheless very imposing and quite endearing. We managed to get our bus back to Blisworth with no problems and quietly fiddled around for the rest of the day. We may drift off a little north tomorrow, but time is not of the essence.

Guildhall, Northampton

Tuesday

We lazily woke after nine o'clock to a fresh and breezy morning. We happily pottered for a couple of hours before quietly and slowly making our way north. After a short time we came to a water point and duly joined the queue of four boats patiently awaiting their turn to replenish the water tank. The water tap was just off the main line on the Northampton arm, which eventually leads to the River Nene. This effectively means a 90° turn across the wind, and then after filling up with water, the same again, only in reverse. The crosswind here was particularly strong. The attempts of the awaiting boats to get to and, the more difficult task, get away from the water point were most entertaining. For some reason, narrowboat helmsmen seem to have no idea how to handle windy conditions. Admittedly, narrowboats are difficult to manoeuvre, especially if there is any wind or current; however, the skippers seemed to have no concept of how their craft would react to what was, although strong, a fairly constant wind. There was a great revving of engines, whirring of bow thrusters, quick change of gears from forward to reverse and back again, tillers waggling like demented wind vanes and the occasional oath. Still the boats were going in all directions, crashing against each of the canalside and careering into other moored boats before slamming into the water mooring. We learnt from all their mistakes and had no shame about using mooring ropes and a deal of heaving to get where we wanted to go and back again. We only travelled five miles before mooring up for the evening at Bugbrooke opposite The Wharf Pub. Bugbrooke is another very pretty Northamptonshire village set about half a mile back from the canal. It has mostly large, well maintained houses built in the typical light brown stone of this area. A fair number of these houses were thatched and of the postcard variety. The village is also mentioned in the Domesday Book and is dominated by its 13th century church (again no photo). It sports one post office, three shops and four pubs. That's not a bad ratio.

Bugbrooke residence and me

Wednesday

This week is taking on a surreal atmosphere as we have only to average four or five miles a day (there are no locks until the last two days) and even then we will arrive in Braunston too early. We have to deliberately do everything in slow motion. We rise late, take an age to eat breakfast and even longer to clear up the dishes. We stop at every village within walking distance, and there are not many, and take an inordinate interest at any canalside view, shop, boat, sheep, cow, cuddly toy, anything at all. This morning was cold and windy. We left Bugbrooke mid-morning and it was not long before we stopped on the outskirts of Nether Heyford. This is yet another pretty Northamptonshire village with large, well maintained houses in typical light brown stone. You have heard all this before; just re-read the description of Bugbrooke and it applies equally well for Nether Heyford. The inhabitants seem a well moneyed lot, albeit friendly natives.

At least Nether Heyford was about a mile from the canal, so the walk there and back served to fill in the time to lunch as well as contributing to our aggregate walking total of three miles a day. The next highlight was mooring up after lunch to fill up with water. We managed to spin this out for about an hour before setting off for the village of Weedon. I think you already have the description for villages in this area so I will not repeat it. We moored up mid-afternoon, having managed to travel all of four miles in four hours. However, just as I turned off the engine we received a phone call from our Milton Keynes friends, Lyn and Neil. They had just got back from their wedding in the USA (well not theirs but one of Lyn's nephews). As they were going up to Cumbria tomorrow, were we close, and could they visit, like now? We had to think for all of a nanosecond before saying "yes" and "yes". They duly arrived with an Indian take away (vegetarian). We spent a really pleasant evening eating curry (vegetarian), drinking a few glasses of wine and generally chewing the fat; well, we have known them for thirty years.

Very old residence at Weedon

Thursday

Once again we woke (late) to a cold windy morning. The forecast was to get sunny and warmer weather in the afternoon and we did. We cast off and got the washing machine going as we cruised slowly along. The plan for the day was to go all of five miles, but this time there were seven locks to ascend in the last half-mile. All went according to plan. There were no villages at all to view today, but we did stop at a marina at the foot of the Buckby seven lock ascent for a few basic provisions and a pump out (well, the Henderson family had visited). We were joined by another narrowboat to go through the locks. The gentleman and his wife looked about sixty years old. He wore a flat cap and for all the world could have been a Cumbrian farmer. She was a little more exotic, but only because she came from the Bahamas. However, and get this, their narrowboat was pink and was called *Comfortably Numb*. Not in my wildest dreams would I have thought they were Pink Floyd fans. On chatting, we established that they had in fact bought the boat a year ago from a live-aboard. Our experience is that live-aboards fall into three distinct groups: i) the middle-aged couple who have sold up their house and are enjoying each other's company (or not) whilst spending their kids' inheritance; ii) the young couple who stick around an area whilst going to work every day, using their boat as a base; and iii) the hippies of the canal system who may or may not stick around, certainly do not go to work every day, and look as if they have not any inheritance to pass on and have bought various substances with any inheritance that has been passed to them. These chaps and chapesses of group iii) are a throwback to the 1980s and are commonly known by us shiny boat brigade as "scruffies" (well, not by me, but I can understand why). Clearly *Comfortably Numb* was bought from a deranged live-aboard (could you live in a pink boat?) and our Cumbrian farmer look-alike had no idea who Pink Floyd are, or indeed the source of inspiration for their songs. That was the juxtaposition and the dichotomy: a pink psychedelic boat inhabited by a flat-capped sexagenarian and his wife. They had booked their boat repaint next month (not pink) but hadn't decided whether to change the name. I personally think he should stick with *Comfortably Numb;* apart from being unlucky to change the name of a boat, what a great name. I wish I had thought of it.

Above the Buckby locks is Norton Junction, where the Leicester line branches off to the north and the main line continues west to Braunston. We stopped for the day at the junction, which was quite busy with boats although there are no villages or towns in the area. There was however, a pub called the New Inn at the top lock-side (I guess it would have been new about a hundred years ago). Pam and I went for a long walk along the canalside and through the fields and thoroughly enjoyed it. We visited this quaint pub admiring this throwback to another age and marvelled at how it could survive being in the middle of nowhere and miles from any conurbation. Then I discovered it had its very own WiFi hotspot network and better still, it was free. Never judge a book by its covers.

New Inn with its very own WiFi

Friday

We had a slight change of plan today. Instead of the intended journey of some two miles, we stayed put (the WiFi facility at the pub contributed to this change of mind). We did a little bit of a reconnoitre of our intended journey by walking across the fields for a couple of miles to the village of Welton, had a drink at its only pub (no shops) called The White Horse, and then walked back via the canal. This was well in excess of our daily three mile requirement, so I shall bank the excess miles for a rainy day. Welton, although a Northampton village, does not have the template description which I have bored you with on previous days. It has more modern houses, although the old village centre does fall into the mould. In its centre is a church which was built in 1245. Whilst we were admiring it from the lane, a lady (perhaps she was a warden) came out of it, gaily announced it was open should we wish to have a look around, and then she drove off in her little car. We poked our noses around the door to see if any silver had been left and what other goodies were on display. Now as you have gathered, I like churches. However, this is limited to the outside. Pam, on the other hand, prefers the inside, not to worship, or anything like that, but just to look at the wooden carvings, the stained-glass windows, any silver plates that may have been left lying around and generally soak in the atmosphere. Welton church had all of these in buckets, and not a soul around – very trusting indeed. In the UK we usually have some kind of memorial in churches dedicated to those from the parish who perished in the World Wars. The Great War normally has a far longer list than WWII, but I guess if you are on either list, this nicety is a little academic. Anyway, there were six men from the parish of Welton who died in the Great War, and an unbelievable four of them came from the same family. That seems very unfair to me. I am sure there is a story to be told here.

Welton Church

Saturday

The hot, sunny weather was back: not the oppressive humid heat of late, but an English summer day. We pottered for a bit, drank coffee, picked up my e-mails at the New Inn (of which I had a couple) and reluctantly left late morning. We enjoyed this little neck of the woods, even if there was nothing here. We decided to try to get a daily paper so, wait for it, took a right turn up the Leicester branch and cruised for a couple of miles before reaching Watford Gap service station. Now most people duck off the M1 motorway for a coffee, paper or a bit of a kip in their car, white van, articulated lorry, etc. – not us. We arrived in a narrowboat. Pam hopped over a little fence, crossed the car park and returned two minutes later clutching my *Daily Telegraph*. It was here we saw a Rough-Legged Buzzard circling overhead. Now this is not a tick; it is very rare and only the second one I have seen. Whilst it was quite easy to spot, I am chuffed that I recognised it and gave myself a huge pat on the back. Having got our paper from the only retail outlet within a ten-mile radius, we retraced our steps (well, hardly steps, more of a wake) and this time continued up the main line of the Grand Union Canal to moor for the day just short of the Braunston Tunnel. After a mega read of all the sections of the Saturday paper, a little spruce-up of the paintwork on *Free Time* and our statutory gin and tonic, we walked up into Welton again, which was about a mile away. They had a bread-and-butter pudding you could kill for.

Me relaxing (again)

Sunday

This morning was idyllic. We were moored in a deep wooded glade just in front of the Braunston Tunnel. The morning was warm and sunny with the rays of sunshine shimmering on the surface of the water through the filter of the leaves on the trees. We are now accustomed to our late rises and leisurely breakfasts. As it was Sunday, we have the added delight of *The Archers* omnibus on the radio. Having consumed coffee and digested *The Archers*, we set off to immediately enter the Braunston Tunnel. This tunnel is just over a mile long. It was dug by Irish navvies, who started at both sides of the hill with the fond wish that they would meet in the middle. Wrong! They missed by about ten feet which necessitates a chicane in the middle of the tunnel. The tunnel is high and wide enough for two narrowboats to pass with a bit of a squeeze. No problem then, unless of course you meet a boat at the aforesaid chicane. Not content with Sod's Law we did not meet one boat at this stage, we met two. However, with good humour, dead slow speed and a bit of a wriggle, we passed without incident. The canal was busy this morning as we passed no less than five-and-a-half boats in the mile-long tunnel. The half boat was in the last hundred meters when we thought we were through and could plainly see daylight to aim for. However, the last boat was crewed by trainee kamikaze pilots who were lurching from side to side and did not look at all in control. I slowed to almost dead stop and was well over to my side of the tunnel but was still well and truly bounced from boat to tunnel, wall and back onto their boat. I was not impressed. Instead of the customary "good morning", stony silence reigned and I also gave them a bit of a glare (this was a bit futile in the darkness, but it made me feel better). On exiting the tunnel we almost immediately joined the queue for the six lock descent into Braunston village. It was at this stage that we fully discovered the damage done to the paintwork by the aforementioned kamikaze boat. Pam spent the afternoon with sandpaper and a paintbrush (well, *Free Time* is having her hull blackened tomorrow, and it wouldn't do to put her into dry dock to be painted in need of a paint, would it?). The descent into Braunston was without incident, if very busy, with boats going in both directions. We moored up early afternoon at the dry dock, reported in and then went off for a wander around the village. Braunston is one of the more famous canal centres, with three or four boatyards, three chandlers, a marina, a post office, a butcher's shop, a small supermarket (with cash-back), four pubs and a small hotel. We had to decide where to have dinner. It was between the Chinese restaurant based in one of the pubs, traditional home-made pub fare in another pub, or a carvery at the hotel. As we will be staying at the hotel for a couple of days, and a Chinese restaurant operating from somewhere called The Wheatsheaf does not sound very authentic to me, the traditional pub grub at The Old Plough (est. 1672) seems to have shaded it.

Grand Union Canal

W/c Monday 7th August 2006

Pam concerned about walking the plank

Monday

We had an early start to the day as we had to go back up to the last lock to get access to the dry dock. Now "back" is the operative word. The canal is too narrow to turn around, so we literally had to reverse back up into the lock, fill the lock with water and then back up to the dry dock. We then drove forward into the covered dock, positioned *Free Time* in the middle of the bay and then drained the bay of water, leaving *Free Time* high and dry (see picture above). This was all very exciting. It has been two years since *Free Time* was launched so she is due her biannual bottom-blacking. Apart from "bottom-blacking" sounding rude, I can never remember whether "biannual" means every two years or twice a year, but it is the former I mean. We packed our little case and walked the half-mile along the towpath to the Millhouse Inn where we were staying for a couple of nights. Apparently, in the interests of economy, some people stay aboard during the blacking process, but I can't imagine Pam standing for this. As you can't run the engine there will quickly be no electric power, the bay is Stygian-like to say the least, and you cannot use any water as it will run out down the freshly painted, still-wet, hull – not ideal. Anyway, the Millhouse Inn is a fairly modern anonymous canalside establishment, and whilst not historic in any meaning of the word, is adequate and quite comfortable. We are looking forward to having numerous baths and unashamedly watching hours of television without concern for signal reception or keeping a weather eye on the state of batteries.

The Millhouse Inn

Tuesday

Now, to be frank, The Millhouse Inn is not great; in fact, it is pretty bad. The downstairs bar areas are fine, but the bedrooms are a disgrace. The carpet should be condemned, you cannot see the television from the bed as it is placed around the corner of an L-shaped room, and worst of all, there is no radio. No *Archers* for a few days then. However, as it is not so much a case of "no room at the inn", as more of a case of "the only inn in town", it is Hobson's Choice. We did, however, have a very good night's sleep; despite promises of watching television into the wee small hours, I promptly fell asleep shortly after nine o'clock, and only awoke at eight. Breakfast was entertaining as an extended family who were the only other guests were complaining loudly to the poor waitress that the rooms were awful (true), that the bath was too small (well ours wasn't) and the shower did not work (ours did). So, the moral of the story is no matter how bad things get, there is always someone worse off. Did I mention the sour milk they got for their cereal?

We took a bus into the nearby town of Daventry. The only reason I had ever heard of it before was the fact that there is a Ford Motorcar plant there. This is a strange little town. It has three major supermarkets in the middle of town. However, it does not have a single restaurant which isn't either Indian or Chinese. The most astonishing thing, wait for it, is that it does not have a single bookshop or newsagent. Can you imagine a town of, say 30,000 people, without a bookshop or newsagent? Supermarkets, although convenient, have a lot to answer for. Having said that, we had lunch in a very elegant Moot Hall (what exactly is a Moot Hall?) in one of the four Indian restaurants. They were doing businessmen lunches (well, I was one once) at a reasonable price. I had a spinach dish (sag) and Pam had a chicken korma. They were excellent and the service was great, the fact we were the only punters in town perhaps going some way to explain why there are no other restaurants in town. We did a bit of shopping and, on returning to Braunston, walked along the canal to *Free Time* to drop the shopping off on the boat. She was looking very smart with her bottom freshly blacked. There was still another coat of paint to be put on, so we will pick her up tomorrow afternoon. The big decision today was which pub to eat in tonight.

Daventry market square

Wednesday

Brian, our Australian friend who lives in Italy, arrived from Melbourne today. (Confused? Well, he had gone home for a couple of weeks and visited us on his way back from Australia to Italy. Clear now?) We pottered around the hotel, meeting the hourly bus from Banbury. Sure enough, Brain was on the second bus. We had a leisurely, and good, lunch at The Millhouse Inn before making our way to the dry dock to pick up *Free Time*. She was ready, having had her bottom blacked and her engine serviced. I paid the bills (ouch!) and we descended the last lock again to moor up for the day. Brian was pretty tired after his marathon flight from Melbourne and his six-hour journey on the Heathrow to Banbury train involving three changes and the bus from Banbury to Braunston (no change on the bus required, but an hour and a half visiting every village within a five-hundred-mile radius; I may have exaggerated the last bit). We dragged Brian back up into the village to do a little shopping (well, if he will drink Campari, what do you expect?) before allowing him forty winks. We will drag him off to The Admiral Nelson pub for dinner, just to make sure he shakes off his jet lag, you understand.

Brian has had a tough day

Thursday

As we knew Brian's jet lag would have him up and about early, we got up at eight o'clock and had an early (for us) breakfast. This was followed by a walk into the village to get the food for lunch and dinner. We cast off at ten o'clock on a cold, cloudy and windy day. Brian quickly took control of the tiller, and we could not prise it off him for the rest of the day. We edged our way out of Braunston, which was incredibly busy with boats, both moored and moving. Once clear of Braunston, we turned north and left the Grand Union Canal to join the northern part of the Oxford Canal. Whilst cruising along I got chatting to a chap who was walking along at the same pace. He was from New Zealand and had just retired. He and his wife were spending four years on a boat in the UK. I asked him how he managed to get a visa for that period. He told me that as one of his grandparents was born in the UK, he was entitled to a four-year visa. He then informed me that if one of my grandparents was also born in the UK, I too could have a four-year visa. I am not sure what nationality he thought I was. We descended three twin narrow locks, which were quite busy and good fun, although we were accosted by a woman from the boat behind us who had taken her dog for a little bit of a stroll. This woman was pleasant enough, but could she talk. After a non-stop monologue about anything and everything, Brian and I looked at each other before muttering apologies and escaping to a discreet distance away, unashamedly leaving it to Pam to remain and politely listen to yet more continuous drivel.

This part of the Oxford Canal is lock free, and although not stunningly pretty, does hold interest. As it is now peak season for holidays, there were quite a lot of boats on the move. We were being tailgated a little by another narrowboat. Now the etiquette on the canal is to allow the following boat to pass by signalling your intention, pulling over to the right, slowing down and allowing the following boat to pass at a sedate speed in a controlled fashion. We did our bit OK, but as the tailgater overtook us, it increased speed to maximum revs and shot by, creating a huge wash. As we had already pulled well over to the side, the wash had the effect of lifting *Free Time* and depositing her on a mud bank at the side of the canal. Our speedster friends waved gaily as they careered by and thanked us profusely without even realising the problems they had caused. After a bit of huffing and puffing and a lot of heaving we got ourselves free and continued our journey. An hour later we passed the said tailgater as he had stopped to fill up with water. He pulled out behind us and proceeded to tailgate once again. Well, you can guess the story. We politely pulled over, tailgater shot by doing ten zillion revs and *Free Time* was left high and dry, again. We were not happy bunnies. I got my calculations slightly wrong and did not realise that to stop anywhere near a pub, we had to continue travelling to after seven o'clock. It was getting cold, so out came the anoraks, even if it was mid-August. We finished our day at a tiny village called Ansty. Although we ate on the boat, we wandered up to The Rose and Castle pub after dinner for three cappuccinos. We have promised Brian an early night so he could catch up on his sleep. I didn't admit to him that although half past ten may be an early night for him, it is my normal bedtime.

Now what kind of cow is this?

Friday

Regretfully it was once again cold and windy. I blamed Jonah, Brian. Also, once again Brian held onto the tiller with a vice-like grip and steered all the way to our destination, the fair city of Coventry. The rural nature of the Oxford Canal quickly changed when we turned onto the Coventry Canal to cruise into the centre of the city. We did not meet a single boat on the two-hour trip into Coventry, save for a British Waterways work boat which was pulling out rubbish from the canal. This did not bode well. The suburbs, all four miles of them, are not, in common with most city suburbs, particularly attractive but also not without interest. The terminus is situated in a modern, secure and quite attractive basin which was full of boats. We managed to shoehorn ourselves into the last space. The city centre was a ten-minute stroll. Coventry is a strange city. To be frank, it leaves a lot to be desired. I guess being flattened by German bombers during the war has not helped any heritage trail or fostered planning to preserve the old culture of pre-war Coventry. I suspect that the climate of the age when they were re-building Coventry was to sweep away the bomb-shattered areas and rebuild decent homes in the modern architecture. However, what might have been attractive in the early 1950s cannot be deemed attractive by today's standards. This is epitomised in the cathedral area. The old cathedral was destroyed in 1941. The building shell still remains and, indeed, today the site is serene, atmospheric and very attractive, with grassy areas and what remains of the walls preserved. The new modern cathedral was built alongside. It has its redeeming features, but frankly is a pale shadow of the original. It just does not have the stature of the traditional building, but nevertheless is a brave attempt to bring in a new order. We had a wander around the transport museum, which specialises in the many car manufacturers which used to be situated in the Coventry area, now sadly long gone. Brian is a bit of a petrol head, so was enthralled by this. He was eventually physically ejected when the museum closed at five o'clock. As usual, the only theatre in town was between productions, so we went off to the cinema in the early evening. We saw Michael Mann's *Miami Vice*, starring Colin Farrell and Jamie Foxx. It was not quite a turkey but bordering on it. The plot was somewhat weak, consisting of our two heroes infiltrating a stereotypical Colombian drug cartel (apologies to Sandra, my Colombian daughter-in-law) as their logistics experts. This, of course, gave the opportunity for lots of scenes of aircraft, cars and boats (called "go fast boats", I kid you not). Anyway, I enjoyed it. The action scenes were good and the whole film was accompanied by a really good musical soundtrack (well, I thought it was, but accept that it might have irritated the hell out of some people). We finished the evening by going to a really good Italian restaurant, quirkily called Kakooti. It is situated in Spon Street. This is one of Coventry's few attractions. The civic fathers decided about thirty years ago to try to preserve all the medieval buildings left in Coventry by dis-assembling (is there such a word?) them *in situ* and re-assembling them all in one street. This is a little odd, and obviously a very artificial attempt at creating a tourist trap, but it is surprisingly effective.

Pam and Brian on Spon Street

The old Coventry Cathedral

Saturday

Sadly, it was cold and windy yet again. I think the story of it being a really hot summer until now was wearing a bit thin for Brian. We headed north again, back through the four miles of suburbs. However, this time at the Oxford Canal, we hung a left and continued up the Coventry Canal. Brian continued to hang onto the tiller for grim death, but he was a natural at helming (must be something to do with flying light aircraft for an awful lot of years). We confidently left him in charge whilst reading papers and drinking coffee in the warmth of the main cabin. We stopped for lunch on the boat on the outskirts of Bedworth before continuing to Nuneaton. The canal is a little distance away from the town centre, so we happily walked the twenty minutes through a residential area before reaching the town centre. Now I know the UK has 1.5 million Muslims, and I think we saw 1.4 million of them in Nuneaton. The gentlemen were without exception ultra-polite as we had to elbow our way through crowds of people on the pavement. The ladies in black did not say a lot. Nuneaton is, in the words of our guide book, "a typical Midlands town". It is entirely without charm, more than a little run down and not helped by the so-called market traders who inhabit the main street in the shopping area with their proliferation of white vans. The only redeeming factor was Costa Coffee, and even there the tables could do with a good clean. We didn't stay long, but pushed on to Hartshill, mooring at The Anchor Inn. Pam produced an excellent dinner, and we retired to the pub for coffee and a chat.

Pals together

Sunday

It rained heavily overnight and well into the morning. Undaunted, we stayed in bed until about ten o'clock, but managed to get up in time for *The Archers* omnibus. Brian assumed pole position as helmsman (again) and off we set once the rain had dispersed. The canal had become more rural and, indeed, a deal prettier. We travelled through quarry country with its man-made spoil heaps (now landscaped), but they weren't overly intrusive. We arrived at Atherstone, which also is the start of an eleven lock descent. The locks are narrow gauge, so quite dinky, and we proceeded to zoom through them. Midway down the flight, I left the team to go to a local supermarket because, horror of horrors, we had run out of red wine. The little I saw of Atherstone was impressive, with an attractive main street with attractive shops, not dissimilar to Cockermouth. Having got the red wine, we proceeded to drink half of it for lunch on board, before completing the descent of the locks and eventually stopping for the night at Poleworth. I insisted that we went for a walk to the abbey. It is 10th century with a modern extension (I guess 16th century) but one wonders how on earth they got planning permission from whomever was in charge of planning then and how many groats had to pass under the table to enable permission to be granted. It is such an out-of-character building connected by a corridor to the abbey. The same issues are prevalent today. Anyway, the splendid gateway and clerestory are still intact. Indeed, Egbert, the first Saxon king, built a nunnery here. We went to the Fosters Yard Hotel to have dinner at their Balti restaurant. Is that incongruous or what? Anyway, the food was excellent.

Polesworth Abbey

W/c Monday 14th August 2006

Free Time

Monday

We didn't have to travel far as our destination was Tamworth, only three miles away. Tamworth is the last town for some time with a railway station, convenient for Brian's departure for Heathrow on Tuesday. The morning started with Brian making porridge, Italian style, for us. Apparently the secret is a combination of using Quaker oats, the amount of salt used, the critical timing of cooking after it reaches boiling point, and serving with cold milk and Demerara sugar; anyway, very good it was. My stomach was duly lined for the day. We fiddled around until eleven o'clock before setting off for our short hop to Tamworth. After a lunch of pasta on the boat (this time Pam was the chef), we walked the twenty minutes into town. Tamworth is quite attractive. It has an ancient history, being the capital of Mercia between the 8th and 10th century. The current civic fathers have made an effort with the gardens surrounding the Norman castle. It also has an imposing church and a very fine Town Hall which was built in 1750, the site of a Charles Dickens public reading of some of his novels. We walked to the train station to check out the train timetable for Brian's journey the following day. We were entertained by a loud yobbish lad who announced he was going to commit suicide. He asked whether anyone could give him a last cigarette. The station staff informed him in no uncertain terms that the station was a no smoking zone. He was a little miffed about this, so walked out, cigaretteless, to stand defiantly in the middle of the railway track. He then proceeded to inform his audience that he was going to kill himself as no one liked him (hardly surprising as he was obviously an attention-seeking, loud lout; well, I didn't like him). He proceeded to bring a train to a halt for quarter of an hour (I guess we can add a trainload of delayed commuters to those who don't like him as well). The station staff were like a well-oiled machine. They made a phone call to the police, halted any through train traffic and then steadfastly refused to get involved. The boys and solitary girl in blue arrived promptly in three cars and proceeded to arrest the moron. Hopefully he will be locked up for some considerable time. Brian and I were as one on this, although Pam was a lot more sympathetic. We had a straw poll of the onlookers. If Tamworth station had been the Coliseum in ancient Rome, I am afraid the thumbs down would have had their gory way. We spotted a carvery in a hotel in town, so we will treat Brian to the delights of traditional roast beef and Yorkshire pudding this evening.

Tamworth Town Hall

Tuesday

The day started early, and I mean early. The various alarm clocks and telephones went off at an incredible six o'clock. Brian's train from Tamworth to catch his plane at Heathrow left at half past seven. The station was a thirty-minute walk away, hence the unearthly hour. We got up, not without both effort and a grumble, and walked with Brian to say our fond farewells on the railway platform. Brian was the perfect guest. He was good company, not demanding, and above all, did not snore. Pam and I got back to the boat just after eight o'clock and set off. We zoomed through a couple of locks in the first quarter of an hour. With Brian hogging the tiller for the last week, we almost had to learn how to helm again. The dominant buildings on the skyline of Tamworth are the castle and its church. Both the castle tower and the church steeple can be seen for miles around. We set off from the east of the town, heading south to the junction of the Birmingham and Fazeley Canal, and then north-west on the last leg of the Coventry Canal. We almost circumnavigated the town, so two hours later we were still within spitting distance of those damned blots on the horizon. We stopped at Fradley Junction for lunch. This is where the Coventry Canal ends and the Trent and Mersey Canal begins. It was busy, with boats everywhere. There are elegant British Waterways workshops, a flight of five narrow locks, a pub called The Swan, and a number of large houses with well kept grounds tumbling down towards the canal. There were also about a zillion spectators (gongoozlers in canal speak) snapping away with their digital cameras and to a man (or woman) hoping for some almighty cock-up as boats weaved in and out trying to avoid each other, avoid moored boats on both side of the already narrow canal, and avoid the lock walls on entry and exiting – no pressure there then. The Trent and Mersey here is very attractive. We decided to put some miles on the clock and eventually moored up at seven o'clock (well, it was *Archers* time) in a pretty wood at Wolseley Bridge. There is a pub, a garden centre and a craft centre. We shall explore tomorrow as we are both shattered by the early start and the long day, mitigated by the impressive twenty-six miles, five locks and one removable bridge.

Trent and Mersey Canal

Wednesday

Well, when we eventually got up, explore we did. We walked up to the garden centre to find there was also an English Nature Reserve beside it. We walked around the reserve, bought a couple of Busy Lizzies at the garden centre and walked across the road to the craft centre, which consisted of a number of very old buildings with antique shops, picture framers, art galleries and general old tat for sale. The whole experience was very enjoyable. We only cruised for about an hour before stopping for lunch in the grounds of Shugborough Hall. I managed to negotiate a concessionary entrance fee on the argument (not that we argued, of course) that we were retired. Pam was embarrassed but I was chuffed, especially as I saved £6. Now in case you didn't know (and I didn't), Shugborough Hall (and extensive grounds) was the family home of the Ansons, aka. the Earls of Lichfield. They came upon hard times and were unable to pay death duties when Patrick Lichfield became the fifth Earl in the 1960s. He had to turn over his ancestral home to the government in lieu of payment and it is now run by the National Trust. We spent a very enjoyable afternoon wandering around the hall, servants' quarters, farm and garden. In the 19th century they employed a French chef at an annual salary of £105, the cook was paid £25 and the third maid was given clothes and keep (no money). The attitude of this family is summed up by two examples of crass, single-minded selfishness. There is a letter from the fourth Earl (now that was in the 20th century) congratulating his head gardener on his excellent service in providing the family with vegetables, fruit and cut flowers all the year round and for training his staff to not be seen! They also bought up the old village of Shugborough on a piecemeal basis and demolished each building purchased to give them more privacy. That said, I always thought Patrick Lichfield played on the fact he was a cousin of the Queen and that he was only a well-connected rich boy who bought the best equipment available to take snapshots. There was an exhibition of his work on display. It was amazing. The composition, contrast and sheer imagination in each of his photographs was breathtaking. I take it all back. He was a very talented photographer.

The day was warm and indeed, the sun came out in the afternoon. For the first time for over a week, the shorts were put on and the knees came out. We left Shugborough late afternoon to chug north up to Weston-on-Trent. This village is very pretty, with a sympathetic mixture of large cottages and new housing. Our mooring was enlivened by a colony (flock?) of guinea-fowl, who literally seem to rule the roost in this area. They live on both sides of the canal and quite happily used the road bridge to get from one side to the other. Why did the guinea-fowl cross the road?

Shugborough Hall

Thursday

The day was overcast (again), but warmer than of late, so the knees remained out. The Trent and Mersey Canal is winding, narrow, rural and very pretty. The two locks we ascended were spaced out, allowing time for showers, hair drying, clothes washing and reading en route. On the second lock, we met a Liverpool Boat (*Free Time* was also built by Liverpool Boats) descending at the same time. On chatting we compared notes on Liverpool Boats, as both our boats were of a similar age. It transpired that the chap was having some minor problems with his electrics, but was unable to obtain the electrical drawings (he bought his boat second hand). With a flourish I produced the schematic drawings which were in my owner's manual. I got huge brownie points and managed not to give away the fact that I had no clue what any of the lines or squiggles on the drawings meant. We arrived at the small town of Stone by early afternoon.

We had been in Stone a couple of times before over the years and liked it immensely. It is small enough to be cosy, but large enough to have all the normal facilities (cinema excepted) that a town should have. Pam and I separated for a couple of hours and wandered around quite happily doing our own thing. For me that consisted of library for internet, bookshop because I like them and wine merchant because we had run out of red wine. Pam, I had no doubt, was shopping for clothes, food and a paperback book. Luckily she only returned with two out of three, the last two. It rained heavily for a couple of hours in the late afternoon, but that was OK as we were safely tucked up inside watching everyone getting wet at the next lock, which is only 100 yards away. We ate on board and then went to The Star Inn, which is alongside the aforementioned lock. This is a superb traditional lock side pub dating from the 14th century, which is obviously well before the canal which was built in 1775. The other thing about this pub is that the many rooms are all on different levels – no good for wheelchairs then. Indeed, it is apparently in the *Guinness Book of Records* as having more different levels than any other pub (I know this because it is on a plaque on the outside wall).

PS. In last Thursday's journal I showed a picture of an odd looking cow (reproduced on the next page). I had no idea what type it was but am now reliably informed by Uncle John (who is never wrong and apparently actually reads the journal) that it is an Old English Longhorn, an ancient breed which almost became extinct until it was saved by some farmers dedicated to preserving these old breeds.

Stone High Street

Now what kind of cow is this?

John says it is an old English Longhorn

Friday

The weather forecast was fine for the morning with heavy prolonged rain for the afternoon. We had a cunning plan to combat this: we would leave Stone by nine o'clock and arrive in Stoke-on-Trent early afternoon. Now we kept our part of the bargain, but the weather perversely was very, very wet in the morning and fairing up to a nice sunny afternoon. Undaunted, we donned our waterproofs and off we went. Progress was steady. I managed to steer Pam past the Wedgwood Pottery Showroom without stopping. The outskirts of Stoke were the usual urban sprawl, but enlivened by the old pottery kilns which are now being preserved. We encountered a hired boat hurtling around a blind corner on the wrong side of the canal. We took evasive action and promptly found ourselves stuck on rocks at the side of the canal. A boat following us also experienced the same fate. The helmsman of the hire boat smiled apologetically and claimed his tiller had jammed. Well, if you believe that, it would explain being on the wrong side of the canal, but I think it too much of a co-incidence to believe his throttle cable had jammed at maximum as well. We dusted ourselves off, pushed the boat off the rocks with a pole and happily the sun came out at this point. We dried everything off by switching on the central heating and draping the various radiators with wet clothes. Our next adventure was to knock a rather expensive bottle of Barbera d'Asti over which was half full, regretfully to become completely empty. Now get this, the wonderful aromatic fumes from the spilt wine set the gas alarm off. Health and Safety being what it is today, you cannot turn the alarm off. Despite opening all the doors and windows and cruising at a hundred miles an hour to create a draft through the boat, the alarm buzzed and buzzed. It was driving me nuts. An hour later I resorted to taking it apart only to find it is hard-wired into the electrics. Out came the soldering iron to un-hard-wire it. Just at that stage the alarm stopped. I wonder if some cheap plonk would have had the same effect. We stopped near an entertainment complex which consisted of Odeon cinemas and ten-pin bowling. We gave the bowling a miss and went to the cinema. Now out of the seventeen films showing, we had seen six of them, decided to give such gems as *Snakes on a Plane*, *Kabhi Alvida Naa Kehna*, and *Nacho Libre* a miss, which only left cartoons for nine-year-olds, tripe like *John Tucker Must Die* and a somewhat obscure film called *Akeelah and the Bee; Akeelah and the Bee* it was then. Pam and I were the entire audience. Not another soul was in the cinema. They did not even bother to show any adverts or trailers. The projectionist must have decided we were not worth it. The film was directed by Doug Atchison and starred Lawrence Fishburne. It is a simplistic tale about an eleven-year-old black girl from the Los Angeles ghetto, played by Keke Palmer, with her mum being Angela Bassett, who entered the National Spelling Bee – Akeela that is, not her mum. On the way to winning (oops, have I given away the ending?) she managed to unite her dysfunctional family, her poverty-stricken community, the local bad lads in the 'hood and an angst-ridden English professor (Laurence Fishburne). Now perhaps I am a complete cynic, but I would also add that the film was amusing and had a massive "feel good" factor. It certainly deserved a larger audience. We had a meal at the local Toby Inn before retiring for an hour of television watching and journal writing.

Pottery Kiln, Stoke-on-Trent

Saturday

Sadly, it was cold and drizzly yet again. We set off at nine o'clock in search of diesel, water and a pump out (these are the three items we seemed to constantly keep an eye on). Half an hour later we arrived at a boatyard. The fuel berth was already occupied by a beat-up old narrowboat. I decided to come alongside this boat to go in search of someone from the boatyard. Just as we were coming alongside, one of the curtains on the boat opened with a cantankerous old man's face glaring out of it and demanding to know what we were doing. When I explained that we were coming alongside to get fuel, he said we weren't as he had painted his handrails last week. Now this was all very strange and un-boatman like, as coming alongside is common practice in congested areas. As his boat was obviously resident there, I can only assume he had something to do with the boatyard, so decided that if that was the welcome, I would be better spending my money elsewhere. Harecastle Tunnel was our next adventure. Harecastle was completed in 1777 after eleven years' construction. It is 2,926 yards long, 9 ft wide and in the middle very, very low. The water here is orange, due to local ironstone leaching into the canal. As it is only 9 ft wide, lock-keepers at both ends control the traffic. Usually this involves a wait of about an hour or so to allow the tunnel to clear of boats coming one way before boats going the other way are allowed through. I thought this would an opportunity to fill up with water from the tap at the entrance. No chance; as we arrived we passed two boats coming South and were waved straight through by the lock-keeper (I guess that should be tunnel-keeper) as the fifth and last boat heading North. Harecastle Tunnel is particularly eerie as well as being reputedly haunted by the "Kidsgrove Boggart". As you gingerly penetrate the gloom of the tunnel, the doors are slammed shut after you throwing you suddenly into the pitch black. This is done to assist the forced ventilation generated by enormous extraction fans. For the next three quarters of an hour, we were buried deep beneath Harecastle Hill, but secure in the knowledge we would not meet a kamikaze boat coming the other way. At the Northern portal, Kidsgrove, we left the Trent and Mersey Canal to join the Macclesfield Canal. The slightly quirky thing about the junction is that the Macclesfield is a very sharp turn to the left, not to the right as you would expect as we wanted to head north-east. All was revealed in the next few hundred yards as our route looped around from west to the north and crossed over the top of the Trent and Mersey which had conveniently ducked under by descending via a couple of locks – all very confusing and very clever. Our next stop was at The Heritage Narrowboats. Ann and John may remember this boatyard as the one from which we hired a narrowboat some years ago. It now has a swish marina extension. Here, we got a proper welcome, encouraged to come alongside a boat which was in the fuel berth. We were filled with diesel and emptied of sewage with a smile and a chat. We stopped in the early afternoon at Congleton. Although the rain persisted, we had a walk into town. The walk from the canal is along a number of bridle paths which emerge in the town centre. The town is typical Cheshire: pretty, moneyed and quite quaint. It has 29,000 souls, so is not huge. Surprisingly, it does have a theatre. Not surprisingly they are between shows. I guess we will read the papers, watch a little television and perhaps wander into the Wharf Inn for a nightcap in the knowledge that I can WiFi at the same time. I know this because Garry rang to tell me the football score (1-1 with St. Mirren after being robbed by a diabolical refereeing decision of chalking off a perfectly good Aberdeen goal and letting in, again, a last-minute goal. Not that we are biased) and to tell me the names of the pubs in Congleton with WiFi. The boy is a star.

Harecastle Tunnel

Sunday

It rained very heavily overnight and well into the morning. I was up and about by eight o'clock, leaving Pam in bed. I set off, and to be fair, Pam produced tea, pomegranate juice and croissants within half an hour, so I guess she got up shortly after me. The morning was wet and pretty horrible. However, nature was out in force. First, we entered a lock and found a roe deer gently floating in it. It was dead, but looked pristine with its red coat and little antlers. I have no idea how it met its end, but it was quite strange locking up with a dead deer floating beside you. After an absence of some time, the birds were out in force. Jays were in abundance, every mile of the canal seemed to have its resident kingfisher, and there was a general chirping at all times. A little male sparrowhawk flew alongside the boat and then flipped over the top of *Free Time* to slam into the hedgerow running alongside the canal on the opposite side. There was a short squeal and then silence as the sparrowhawk clung to the side of the hedgerow. After about thirty seconds, it flew off with a small bird clutched in its talons. It had obviously used *Free Time* as a screen before making its deadly attack on a little blue tit: pretty impressive, unless of course you were the blue tit, which would not be that impressed. The day began to dry out and the sun was trying to put in a guest appearance. The Macclesfield Canal is narrow and shallow, but quite majestic as it makes its unrelenting progress towards the Pennines. The locks on the Macclesfield are grouped together in two major climbs. We ascended the first of these, twelve Bosley Locks, which are in a semi-wooded and semi-pastoral setting. We climbed a total of 118 feet in tranquil and beautiful surroundings, arriving at Macclesfield in the early afternoon. Like Congleton, Macclesfield remains a little aloof and keeps its distance from the upstart of the canal. Undaunted we walked into town along an unpromising route before suddenly coming into the middle of a very passable town. We walked around and picked up a few groceries before returning to the boat. Everything had dried out externally, so I spent an hour mopping out the engine compartment, clearing the drainage channels and generally unblocking the drainage holes which were clogged up with compost from Pam's numerous replantings of the flower boxes. That explained why the bilge pump was working overtime in the rain of last night. The sun was shining and we are all of 100 yards from a pub quirkily called *Puss in Boots,* which reputedly has WiFi. We will visit later this evening, purely in the interests of communication with the family, you understand. If you get this journal tonight (Sunday evening) you will know it does have WiFi and it works; if not, I will trudge down to the library tomorrow.

Macclesfield Canal

W/c Monday 21st August 2006

Free Time

Monday

We walked into Macclesfield first thing to go to the Post Office and the library. By the time we had walked back, filled up with water and had coffee it was eleven o'clock. We had nineteen miles to travel in the day, but no locks. We continued up the Macclesfield Canal, which remained its usual pretty self. The canal, although still on one level, takes on a more rugged appearance as it weaves around hills, strides across valleys on aqueducts and embankments, and generally clings to steeps hillsides. We were indeed approaching the Pennines. There are a number of canalside mills which have been converted to posh offices or apartments. No doubt in their heyday they were dark and satanic; today they are freshly painted and look very desirable. One incongruous sight was a very elegant 18th century cottage (I know this because the date was above the door) with no less than three helicopters parked on the lawn. This is moneyed Cheshire, after all. At the top of the Macclesfield Canal, we took a detour by turning east onto the Peak Forest Canal. This terminates at the twin forks of Whaley Bridge and Buxworth. We cruised up to Whaley Bridge (close to the home of swizzles sweets), turned around in the basin and took the other fork to Buxworth. This is an interesting place. Its original name was Bugsworth, but the good citizens of the village decided that they did not like the bug connotations (perhaps they were called worthy buggers?) and so, in 1930, changed the name to Buxworth. However, the main claim to fame, and indeed the main activity in the area, was centred around the Bugsworth basins. Being traditionalist, the canal folk steadfastly refused to change the name of their basin from Bugsworth to Buxworth, thus creating an anomaly on the map with two spellings, but also effectively rendering the attempted name change ineffective. Bugsworth basins are a complex of canal loading basins built in 1800 to transport limestone from the quarries, some six miles away, to Manchester. Horse-drawn trams conveyed the limestone from the quarries to the basins where it was trans-shipped onto canal boats for wider distribution. The tram tracks are still there and, indeed, this trade continued until 1923. It is an atmospheric and fascinating place, especially as it is relatively remote. We never did see the actual village of Buxworth, but did visit the local pub named The Navigation (there must be at least a million pubs called The Navigation on the canal system). It was OK, but had at least three resident dogs which just seemed to sleep all the time on the chairs allegedly provided for the punters. It was once run by Pat Phoenix, of Elsie Tanner fame, but there is no mention of this in the pub. No wonder it is up for sale.

Macclesfield Canal

Tuesday

We had bright sunshine for a change from the dreary, cloudy, drizzly weather of late. We retraced our previous day's journey of seven miles along the Gowt valley to Marple. All the guide books say that travelling along a canal in the opposite direction is almost like never having been on it before. That is absolutely true. There are all sorts of bits and pieces along the canal banks which I had missed by looking in the opposite direction. Perhaps we should retrace the 820 miles to date to ensure we haven't missed anything. Shortly before lunch we arrived at Marple, which is the site of a flight of sixteen locks which take you down 214 feet alongside the River Goyt. This is when things began to go wrong. British Waterways had closed the flight to effect a repair to No. 5 Lock. It was not scheduled to open again until four o'clock in the afternoon. Undaunted, we walked into the town of Marple. We were expecting quite a small village with perhaps a general store and a couple of pubs. We were wrong. It is a very short walk from the top lock and is surprisingly large; it even sports a cinema (more of this later). After some shopping and yet another visit to the library, we returned to the boat for lunch and, with luck, a little siesta. Well, I got lunch, polished a few brasses and was just working out how I could get away with a little lie down, when the locks were reopened two hours ahead of schedule. Off we went. These locks were particularly hard work. As the locks were closed all day, the water levels were low and the paddle gear very stiff. At lock eleven (they start at sixteen and work their way down) the ground paddle was badly bent, preventing it from closing properly and also fouling the gate. I phoned British Waterways for help, but managed to free it enough with a lot of huffing and puffing and gentle banging with the windlass (well, perhaps not so gentle). We got through, just, and then the British Waterways guys arrived, who promptly closed the flight again. As we, and another three boats, were in the middle, we were allowed to continue as it would be dangerous to moor up in the short pounds overnight. We had delays at the original problematic Lock No. 5, which suffered from a badly leaking cill, making it almost impossible to open the gates against the flow of current caused by the leak without the help of at least three or four burly gents to add their weight, muscle and gravitas against the gate. It was with relief that we finally got to the bottom about half past five. We were then told that the canal had been closed a mile further on by the police. Apparently some poor chap had hung himself from a canal bridge. That puts everything into proper perspective, I think. We decided we had had enough for one day, cleaned up and walked back up to Marple to a pasta house. After dinner we went to the Regal Cinema. This cinema was built in 1878 as a mission hall and converted to a cinema in 1923. Not a lot has changed since then, apart from the admission price, I guess. We went to the circle and were shown to our seats by an usherette in uniform and holding a torch – takes you back a bit. The film was Ken Loach's *The Wind That Shakes the Barley*. It is a tale of two brothers who fought with the IRA in 1920 to get rid of the British, only for one of them to feel betrayed when independence did come as the Irish Free State still swore allegiance to the British King and Northern Ireland remained British. The film was too violent for my liking (I just closed my eyes at the very gory bits), but nevertheless is a remarkable attempt at portraying the struggle from an Irish point of view. It has a strong anti-English bias, but not, I suspect, as strong as the English viewer might think. It showed the brutality of the Black and Tans, whose only excuse was that they had been desensitized by their experiences in the trenches at the Somme. The British brutality is mirrored by the ruthlessness of the IRA and latterly by the army of the Irish Free State. *The Wind That Shakes the Barley* deservedly won the Palme d'Or at Cannes this year.

Canal drained for repairs

Wednesday

We set off at seven o'clock (well, I did leaving Pam in bed, but true to form, she produced a bacon buttie and a cup of tea about an hour later). The morning was, as forecast, wet, but with the promise of some sunshine later in the day. There were no locks for at least three hours, so all was quiet and going well until a hire boat pulled out in front of us after an hour of not seeing another moving boat. The hire boat was fine on the straight but painfully slow whenever we approached a narrowing of the canal (frequently) or blind corners (not so frequent, but acceptable). Despite my tailgating them for at least an hour, they steadfastly ignored me and refused to do the done thing, and pull over to let me pass. Pam came up to helm for a bit whilst I went for a shower. She, of course, did the decent thing and throttled back to allow the hire boat some breathing space (I doubt that they noticed). We approached a lifting bridge. Now the convention when one or more boats come to a lifting or swing bridge is for the lead boat to drop off a passenger to open the bridge. The lead boat then moves through and moors up on the other side of the bridge. All the following boats go through and continue on their journey. The bridge is then closed, the passenger rejoins the ex-lead boat and it then cruises off after the other boat(s) and has the benefit of all the work being done at the next bridge. Although Pam was about ten minutes behind, by the time we got to the bridge they were still faffing around. Pam duly and respectfully hung back. Eventually, the silly woman managed to realise that she was winding the handle in the wrong direction and finally lifted the bridge. Right I thought, we would finally get to overtake them and make up some time. However, as the hire boat went through the bridge hole, the stupid woman hopped onto it leaving the bridge up (very dangerous), and us to sort it out and even worse, we were still stuck behind them. I have a good mind to write to their hire company as a "disgusted from Tunbridge Wells". Even Pam was annoyed, which says it all. Luckily, at the next junction they turned left towards Manchester and we turned right onto the Huddersfield Narrow Canal. This canal was built in 1811and abandoned in 1944. Over the next fifty years some of the canal was in-filled. Some of it has housing estates, shopping centres, car parks, et al., built all over it. It was a minor miracle when it was re-opened in 2001. Although most of the canal was restored to its original course, there are brand new areas, diversions and general common sense to make the third Pennine crossing work. This became obvious after only half a mile as we went clean through an Asda supermarket. I kid you not; the canal went straight under the supermarket for a distance of at least 150 yards. Apparently, it was the only way through. This canal is not for the faint-hearted. It has locks, locks and more locks. They are hard work. There is no obvious dropping-off point to work the locks, and the pounds are very shallow indeed. After passing through the somewhat grotty area of Stalybridge, the canal quickly gets into rugged remote countryside as it strides across the Pennines. After some three hours we were only three miles away from Stalybridge, but it was a different world, having climbed sixteen locks, or about 200 feet, and driven through a hill by using Scout Tunnel. Although only 200 yards long, this tunnel is literally hewn out of solid rock – none of your fancy tunnel lining by using bricks or concrete. No, this is naked rock which has been gouged out by blasting and shovelling. We moored up late afternoon at a small village called Woodend. On walking through it we found two pubs (one of which had WiFi), an Italian restaurant, and a solitary shop, sadly closed, and perhaps thirty or forty houses.

Yes, the Huddersfield Narrow Canal is narrow!

Thursday

We awoke to bright sunshine after heavy rain overnight. It gave me a chance to use my new window cleaner's rubber wipe which I had bought at a pound shop (yes, it cost me £1). Within two minutes I had dried off the boat and was ready to go without any danger of a wet bottom from sitting on a rail which was still soaking wet from the rain. In the sunshine, the Huddersfield

Narrow Canal was sparkling against a backcloth of dramatic hills on all sides. It threads its way imperiously searching out the line of least resistance through the difficult terrain. It is a wonderful canal, which in a matter of a few miles, has shaken off the smell of industrial decline and embraced the rural and remote atmosphere of a trans-Pennine crossing. We travelled all of two miles, but ascended seven locks, before we stopped for lunch in the picturesque village of Uppermill. This is a former textile village, but now encompasses the tourist age with an abundance of tearooms, gift shops and trip boats. Nevertheless, it is still an attractive stop and shouldn't be sneered at for moving with the times now that the textile industry in the UK is well and truly dead. We continued after lunch for all of a mile (and three locks) to Dobcross. This is an affluent, although spread out, hamlet. It has no shops, two pubs, a good garden centre, a great countryside centre, and an abundance of spectacular scenery. We moored at its tiny basin alongside another four boats, which are all queuing to go through the famous Standedge Tunnel tomorrow.

Free Time dwarfed by the railway viaduct straddling the Huddersfield Canal and the River Tame

Friday

We had an early start as we were told that British Waterways would meet us at eight o'clock. We were up at seven o'clock anticipating an exciting day, as were all the other boats in the basin. One of the boats should have gone through the Standedge Tunnel on Wednesday, but had engine problems, now fixed. The owner, a stage manager, hoped to get through on today's journey. The tunnel is only open Mondays, Wednesdays and Fridays, and limited to four boats in each direction. We thought British Waterways would make an exception due to this poor chap's circumstances and allow him through with us. No, rules is rules, and despite impassioned pleading by everyone, the

British Waterways men were impervious to begging, so we waved goodbye to him. I have no idea what he was going to do as the next week's passages were fully booked. He may become the modern equivalent of the *Flying Dutchman,* forever haunting the Rochdale Canal. We ascended the final nine locks to reassemble at Diggle (yes, it is a real name). The entrance of Standedge Tunnel is disappointingly low-key and belies the fact that we were about to pass through the longest (3 miles 418 yards), highest (645 feet above sea level) and deepest (638 feet beneath the high point on the moor above) canal tunnel in the world. First of all, a horde of British Waterways guys swarmed onto *Free Time* and encased her with heavy rubber sheets. I had already isolated the gas cylinders and the batteries. As *Free Time* was the tallest of the four boats, we were to lead our little cavalcade. I guess the theory was that in the very tight tunnel, if *Free Time* could get through, then the other three smaller boats would as well. We were hooked up to the electric tug and then, fingers crossed, got into the passenger module. No one is allowed to remain with their boat, although a British Waterways operator stays on each boat to manually fend the boats off the rugged jagged rocks which line the tunnel sides and roof. Pets are also not allowed through the tunnel (sorry, Greg) and have to be walked or driven over the summit top. Off we went for our three-hour trip, starting at the Western portal, like mice going into a mouse-hole and then wriggling their way through a black, very, very narrow tunnel through solid rock. The whole experience was breathtaking and certainly not for the claustrophobic. As *Free Time* was immediately behind the electric tug, I could see exactly how much room there was to spare as she threaded her way through the bowels of the earth. The answer was "not a lot"; indeed, at some stages it was millimetres. We emerged into bright sunshine in the late afternoon. We got on well with the people from the other three boats. They consisted of a couple who were teachers, but complete canal enthusiasts (topics of conversation were limited with them). There was a single-hander who spent half his time in New Zealand. He was very cagey about saying exactly what he did, but I got the strong impression that there was something distinctly dodgy about his past. Finally, there was a mother and daughter team who had recently bought a somewhat beat-up little boat and were having a great time moving it from Cambridgeshire to their mooring at Hebden Bridge in Yorkshire. I believe a lot of bonding was taking place. Off came the rubber matting and on came the spectacles to look for any damage by those nasty jagged rocks. There was a little, but nothing Pam and her magic paintbrush could not cure. There was also a lot of soot which had to be washed off. This is a throwback to the vast quantities of railway engine smoke which used to billow around from the parallel railway tunnel with its interconnecting passages. We all retired to The Tunnel Inn for a meal and a few drinks. Actually the few drinks turned out to be far too many drinks; I guess a reaction to having completed one of the great experiences and a team letting down their collective hair. I was shockingly ill later that night. Pam and I are now on the wagon. I think that will last for a few days to give our livers recuperation time.

Free Time **being prepared for tunnel**

Saturday

It was very difficult getting up after the excesses of last night. However, the British Waterways team arrived promptly at eight o'clock to escort us down the first ten locks. Here the locks are tightly packed, resulting in potential water level problems. The teacher couple were up, but there was no sign of life from our New Zealand gangster or the mum and daughter team. I know the mum and daughter got back, because we walked together back to the boats about midnight, but we did leave the other chap in the pub. Perhaps he was still there in a massive lock-in organised by the obliging landlady... *Free Time* led off again, and we descended a total of twenty-one locks in three miles. The paddle gear was stiff, the gates heavy and the locks deep. By the time we reached Slaithwaite (pronounced "Slough-it"), I was well and truly knackered. My knees ached, my arms ached, my back ached and my legs ached. The only good news was that my head didn't ache, having shaken off my hangover very early in the day with all my exertions. We called it a day at two o'clock and went for a walk through Slaithwaite. This did not take long. It is pleasant enough, with a number of individualistic waterside shops, and the architecture is typical Pennine with the warm light-grey stone being prevalent. We visited a coffee shop, bought a couple of paint brushes in an ancient ironmonger, and generally pottered about the boat in the afternoon. I even managed forty winks with no protest from Pam. We plan to have a quiet evening watching a Merchant Ivory DVD, *Heat and Dust,* with Julie Christie and Greta Scacchi. No critique available yet.

Electric Tug at Standedge Tunnel

Sunday

We set off once again at eight o'clock, knowing we had yet another tough day ahead with difficult, heavy locks raining down on us at regular intervals; in fact, we had twenty-three locks in five miles to do before we finished with the Huddersfield Narrow Canal and moved onto the Huddersfield Broad Canal at, surprisingly enough, Huddersfield. My back had seized up, making it very difficult to put on socks and shoes. Now I know how my dad felt when, latterly, he was not quite so mobile as he had been in his youth. Having taken a couple of painkillers, the pills began to kick in and the aches and pains began to ease as the morning and the lock count progressed. If anything, the locks were harder than the previous day, with a number of faults in the paddles which made it necessary to enlist the help of any passers-by to add weight to the pushing and shoving of the gates against an excessive flow of water. With a lot of brute force we progressed. In one lock we got completely stuck as we entered as we were wedged against a wheelie bin (complete with rubbish) that someone had thrown into the lock. Eventually, we reached Huddersfield basin in the early afternoon and happily collapsed for an hour. We walked into the town centre. It is quite modern. The buildings of Huddersfield University (no, I had never heard of it before either) dominate the area in which we are berthed, but it is all very clean and tidy. We decided to eat out after listening to *The Archers*. When we arrived at the pub, who was there but our New Zealand gangster friend, complete with his third or fourth pint in hand. We had a drink with him and chatted about our relative tribulations of the day, when in walked the mother and daughter bonding team (Penny and Sarah). They were fund-raising for Trees for Life, a scheme to regenerate and restore the Caledonian Forest. They told us that one of the British Waterways guys who took us through the tunnel had pledged £5 on their website. They were completely chuffed, especially as British Waterways staff are so poorly paid. Well, I thought, not as poorly paid as me, who doesn't get a wage at all. This uncharitable thought obviously did not occur to Pam, who produced a note from her purse to also make a donation. Anyway, we all had a convivial dinner together and, no we didn't overindulge in the evil drink, although once again we left our New Zealand gangster friend in the pub at closing time.

Now I have made a couple of comments about "dark satanic mills". I knew it was a quotation from William Blake, but had always thought (because a friend had told me) that it actually referred to Oxford and Cambridge universities turning out maladjusted leaders for our fair nation. Now, whilst I could quite believe this of Blake (but then I am very gullible), I could not find any other reference to this theory. I now think that he was indeed talking about manufacturing mills and their treatment of their workers, but those on the Thames, not "up north". Still, I shall continue to refer to any industrial building north of Watford of being a "dark, satanic mill".

Satanic Mill at Linthwaite being converted to executive apartments

W/c Monday 28th August 2006

Free Time

Monday

I waited until the chandlers in Huddersfield opened at half past nine to buy a couple of fenders to replace the ones that had been torn off in the multitude of locks we had undertaken, and a tin of paint to touch up the various scrapes on poor old *Free Time*. We then set off to complete the Huddersfield Broad Canal. This, as the name suggests, is a wide canal, all of four miles long and with nine reasonably maintained locks. My bad back continues, but with a painkilling pill for breakfast, it seems to ease as the day goes on. By the time we had done with Huddersfield with its multifaceted canals and turned onto the River Calder, I had stopped walking like a half-shut knife and almost had a spring in my step. Rivers, in comparison with canals, are wide, fast-flowing and a little scary. Once you get into "river mode", they are fine as long as you make sure that the water levels are not well above normal. They weren't, despite the showery weather we had had of late. We shared a lock with a boat from The Safe Anchor Trust. The aim of the Trust is to provide free access to the waterways for special needs groups. By this I assumed that this meant both mentally and physically challenged groups. Having read the small print of the pamphlet they gave us, I discovered that special needs groups also include kids who are on probation. I assume this is probation as in handed down by our justice courts, and not kids who are looking for a job crewing the boat and are on a trial period. Indeed, it could be both. I was not sure which particular group they had on board when we met them, but it was just as well we weren't rude to them.

This route is a combination of river and canal navigations with a series of flood locks connecting the two. The few miles between Thornhill and Dewsbury are particularly ugly, with post-industrial decay, spoil heaps and general barrenness prevailing. Then all of a sudden the canal cuts deep into a wooded area of spectacular beauty, culminating in a neat little area with two locks in close proximity. There was a middle-aged chap wandering along the towpath picking up any rubbish which has accumulated. He was obviously not employed to do this but was just being a good citizen. It is such a pity there are not more bods like him around. Tidiness begets tidiness, and unfortunately the antithesis is also true. We stopped for the evening at a place called Horbury Bridge, which is just after the Figure of Three Locks. The latter is a bit of a misnomer as there are only two locks. It obviously should have been called Figure of Two Locks, but somehow that does not have the same ring to it. We will explore Horbury Bridge tomorrow, as once again we were too tired to walk up the hill to the small village (twenty-one locks today), but we did visit the pub, which was only 100 yards away. We asked for coffee. On being told there was only instant coffee available, we changed our minds and had gin and tonics (good move).

The wide River Calder

Tuesday

One of my ex-work colleagues, Alastair, joined us for breakfast. He had driven down from Middlesbrough with some pension documents I had to sign (sadly, not my pension but as a Trustee of the Company pension). We fed him bacon butties and caught up with the news. Alastair left by nine o'clock, so we made the promised walk into Horbury Bridge, which didn't take long. It consists of three pubs, a small general store and nothing else of note. Curiosity satisfied, we were once again on our way on a bright but breezy day. The canal/river navigation is becoming increasingly serious as it scales up to deal with the commercial traffic which is prevalent in the North East. This means even heavier lock gates and paddles (oh, my poor back), until mercifully we move from the Calder and Hebble Navigation to the Aire and Calder Navigation (pay attention now, the names may seem similar, but the waterways are not), which has mechanised locks. A turn of our British Waterways key and pushing three buttons is all you have to do – bliss. We have swapped jobs. Pam now does the locks and I do the helming. She knows a good thing when she comes across it. We arrived at Castleford by mid-afternoon. The visitors' moorings were vastly improved with neatly cut grass since our last visit four months ago. The canalside had been cleared of all the rubbish. Castleford town is a little way, and quite frankly is a bit of a dive. However, it too had improved, but will never be a holiday resort. A quiet night in with yet another DVD to watch is the plan for the evening.

Alastair eating as usual

Oops!

<u>Wednesday</u>

I did a bit of T-Cutting to try to restore some of the damage from the Standedge Tunnel (quite successfully, if I do say so). We really don't have far to go now, so a start at mid-morning seemed in order. We immediately locked down onto the River Aire and cruised in splendid isolation for five or six miles. Well, the splendid isolation was broken at one point as an oil tanker (yes, an oil tanker) passed us, running from the coastal port of Goole up to the oil depot at Castleford for inland distribution. We passed the coal-fired power station at Ferrybridge with its huge gantries and coal handling equipment on the riverside before once again entering a canalised section. I went for a shower and a shave when Pam called down saying she had heard on the VHF radio a warning to a commercial vessel that a narrowboat was heading in its direction. Could it be us the unknown whistle-blower was referring to? "Don't be silly, there must be tens of other narrowboats around," I said. Anyway, Pam throttled right back and hugged the side, and I humoured her and continued shaving. Yes, on a blind corner, what should come around, but a bloody great tanker which would have done damage to our paintwork of which the Standedge Tunnel could only dream. It, too, was at dead slow, so there was no issue there apart from a large slice of humble pie for yours truly. We soon turned north again to rejoin the River Aire. Here it was very much narrower and distinctly meandering in its course. Pam, who was still helming, declared herself quite seasick with all the twisting and turning. At least there was no commercial traffic on this section to worry about. We reached our destination for the day, a small village called Beal. It is situated on a small canal cut which by-passes the weir on the river. We walked around, had coffee in one of the two pubs, The Hungry Fox, before returning to *Free Time* for a bit of afternoon reading. There are no shops at all in Beale, so as provisions are running low (well, we have run out of wine), we will try the other pub, Jenny Wren, for dinner tonight.

It pays to keep a look out!

Thursday

Today was a delight. We started off at ten o'clock and continued our circuitous route on the River Aire. This time I helmed, not, you understand, to prevent Pam's sea sickness, but to allow her to wash and dry her hair. However, I didn't mind; the day was calm, and the scenery and wildlife interesting in this remote part of the river. After an hour we turned onto the Selby Canal. This canal is one of my favourites. The water was clear, the sides blurred with vegetation and not a house or building to be seen. Pam took over helming, and I lazed at the front of *Free Time,* listening to the radio, binoculars at the ready and completely in my own zone, both physically and psychologically. It was bliss. The Selby Canal is a Mecca for wildlife. We had several kingfishers leading the way for the duration of the all-too-short two hours (not at the same time, of course, as they are highly territorial; when one kingfisher reached the limit of his patch, another obligingly took over the "follow my leader" role). We saw another terrapin. Not the dinner plate size of the one we spotted on the Thames, but a good saucer size. It looked extremely happy whilst sun bathing on a log at the side. One wondered whether there were any other terrapins released to the wild on the canal, or whether this was a very lonely amphibian. Well, it did not look lonely, but perhaps he, or she, was putting on a brave face. We stopped at the Selby Boat Centre to fill up with fuel and get a pump out (the Hendersons are visiting tomorrow, so we wanted to be prepared). As the pump out point was on the wrong side of the boat, this involved turning 55 foot *Free Time* in the canal at its widest point, which is 56 feet. This was a tricky manoeuvre, but it was even trickier turning *Free Time* back again, which involved reversing about 400 yards. We moored up in Selby Basin in the early afternoon. I have a soft spot for Selby. Its perimeter is not very promising, with run-down council estates and industrial buildings, but the town centre has an excellent 14th century Benedictine abbey with nice little streets leading from it. We first visited almost exactly two years ago, and there are tangible improvements, not least of which is the waterside development around the river and basin area. It's not exactly Canary Wharf, but definitely an improvement in my humble opinion. We were entertained in the evening by the basin's resident kingfisher. It used the adjacent boat as a fishing platform to go diving after small minnows. It had a surprisingly high success rate. Having caught its fish, it then would fly onto a pontoon and proceed to literally beat the living daylights out of the poor little fish before flying off. I never saw it swallowing a fish, so perhaps it was food for its young, or even presents in the wooing process of the future Mrs. (or indeed Mr.) Kingfisher.

Selby Abbey

Friday

We had arranged for Martyn, the satellite dish man, to meet us at eight o'clock. We had damaged our electronic aerial at the Standedge Tunnel (well, we actually sheered it clean off under a very low bridge, so I guess that could be classed as "damage"). As analogue television is gradually being phased out, I decided to replace the electronic analogue aerial with a detachable digital dish, hence Martyn, who had driven up from Stratford. He fitted the digibox, set up the cabling, set up the portable dish and gave me an idiot's guide on how to tune it into Astra II (not Astra I, you will note) using the satellite finder he also sold me. It worked perfectly with crystal-clear pictures on a multitude of channels, but more later. We had booked to lock down onto the tidal section of the River Ouse at noon. We needed to go fifteen miles north on the Ouse on the tidal section before reaching the first point we could stop at, Naburn. We were the only boat doing this route today, so we sailed serenely up river in splendid solitude. The tides were on neaps (that's weak currents to you and me) so there were no real issues. We locked up onto the non-tidal section of the river at three o'clock. Excitedly I moored up and tried to get my satellite television going. Could I get a signal? No, I couldn't. Hopefully it is something to do with the trees surrounding this very pretty spot, rather than some expensive catastrophic equipment failure. Time will tell. Ann, John and Greg arrived at half past four, which shamed me into stopping fiddling with my new toy. We caught up with the gossip, had dinner on board (there is no pub within a mile) and had an evening stroll in the last of the evening's sunshine. The forecast for tomorrow is horrible, so we made the best of the good weather.

Ann and John looking happy (Greg is hiding)

Saturday

Did I mention the weather forecast for the day was horrible? Well, it was. Wet and very windy from lunch-time was the forecast, and wet and very windy from lunch-time it was. As we were on the River Ouse, the number of places to stop was a bit limited. Also, I did not want to be caught on the river with a lot of rain forecast, as the Ouse has a deserved reputation for flooding. With all this in mind, we left Naburn Lock at half past seven. Surprisingly, everyone was up and about, including Greg, at this unearthly hour. We cruised up an already swollen river to York arriving, along with the rain, mid-morning. We moored up and had a quick wander around to buy food for lunch and a newspaper. Off we set again, when the heavens really opened and the wind was getting close to gale force. I think that was the last I saw of the team. I was helming, in full wet weather gear, whilst Pam, Ann and John sat below. Greg came and sat with me for a while, but even he began to get a bit soggy, so he deserted me for the warmth of the cabin – traitor. Pam stuck her head up at one stage to request that the central heating be turned on. I was not impressed. The river continued to rise, so we had to decide on whether to stay at Linton Lock, which has a floating pontoon, and not a lot else, or run up to Boroughbridge, which is a nice little town. We decided on the latter, but this was quite a long way for one day's journey. Thankfully the rain eased by late afternoon, but the wind increased still further making cruising uncomfortable. We eventually arrived at Boroughbridge at seven o'clock. We parked in the last available mooring and had a stiff gin and tonic. I tried to set up the satellite dish once again, but there was a house inconveniently blocking the signal from Astra II, so I was still not able to get the thing to work. We decided to go to the Indian restaurant for dinner. We apologised to Greg for leaving him on the boat and beat a hasty retreat before we gave in to his accusing and doleful eyes. The only table left in the restaurant was immediately beside a table with four young lads. Although not overtly aggressive, they were loud, swearing quite a lot, and generally not pleasant to be beside. We left the table and tried to order a take away instead, knowing this would please Greg. We were then told that it would be half an hour before the food would be ready, so we agreed on a compromise. We would go to the pub and return in half an hour. If the lads had gone by then (they were currently well through their main course) we would eat in, if not we would take the take away to the boat. In the hotel opposite, on talking to some people we had noticed also leaving the restaurant, we discovered that the four young lads had just returned from a tour of duty in Afghanistan and were only letting off a bit of steam, no doubt quite thankful that they were still around to be able to let off steam. Well, this bit of news made me a bit more sympathetic to their slightly anti-social ways.

Communal paddling class?

Sunday

We were rudely awakened at seven o'clock by a fellow boater who just wanted to let us know that the towpath was under water and we were listing to one side as the boat has risen with the water (about three feet), but of course the mooring lines were fixed, hence the list to one side. I made a simple adjustment to the mooring lines, thought about going back to bed, but the moment had passed, so it was an early breakfast. Although sunny, it was still very windy. We hung around waiting for the river to recede. I was quite happy reading the morning papers, when the same chap knocked on the boat at half past eleven saying that he thought the river have gone down sufficiently to be safe (six inches) and would we like to accompany him to Ripon? It was slightly earlier than I would have wished, but at least we would be travelling in company, so off we went. The river was very swollen with a strong current. It was a case of trying to pick out the eddies in the river and staying out of the main current to make any progress at all. On some of the river corners, it was painfully slow, although the engine was screaming, inching our way forward against the flow of water. We had only to go three miles before the next lock, but this took us two hours. The landing jetties of this lock were also under water, but luckily the lock gates were open so we could drive straight in. The next stage of the river, although also swollen, was relatively easy before we locked up again into the Ripon Canal. We had lunch in sheltered, sunny conditions before completing the last mile to Ripon Marina. We found our berth and it really felt like we were home after our epic journey (well, epic to us in a narrowboat, a mere couple of days drive in a car). The day was sunny, our berth was sheltered from the wind and I got the satellite television to work. A perfect end to our summer cruise.

John and Greg walking the towpath line

John and Greg, having dried out

Well, dear readers, our grey nomad cruise is at an end, so this is the last journal. We left almost five months ago on Thursday, 13th April. We have travelled 940 miles, opened (and closed) 755 locks, swung 73 removable bridges and cruised for 665 hours. The purpose of the journal was to keep in touch with all the family whilst we were away. Our summer cruise was a bit of an unknown to us. Although Pam and I have been married for a great number of years, we have never been with each other day in, day out for any great number of days, limited holiday apart.

Did we argue? Well, perhaps just a little, but nothing that I can remember (Pam may have a different view on this). Our summer cruise was our odyssey. After so many years of constant work with its in-built routine, neither of us quite knew how we would cope with the uncertainty of each day, the confined space, each other's company every day, the lack of baths, etc. We coped very well. The time has flown by and we never regretted it. I hope you enjoyed hearing of our travels. I enjoyed your feedback. Now we will visit the family in person. They have been warned!